A GLOSSARY OF POLITICAL THEORY

A Glossary of
Political Theory

John Hoffman

Stanford Law and Politics
an imprint of Stanford University Press
Stanford, California   2007

Stanford University Press
Stanford, California

© John Hoffman, 2007.

Originating publisher: Edinburgh University Press Ltd

A CIP record for this book is available from the Library of Congress

ISBN-10 0-8047-5727-5 (hardback)
ISBN-13 978-0-8047-5727-0 (hardback)
ISBN-10 0-8047-5728-3 (paperback)
ISBN-13 978-0-8047-5728-7 (paperback)

Typeset in 10.5/13 Sabon by
Servis Filmsetting Ltd, Manchester, and
printed and bound in Great Britain by
Cox & Wyman Ltd, Reading

Contents

Acknowledgements

I am very grateful for the help and advice given to me by Keith Faulks in writing this glossary.

I would like to thank David Cox and Morten Fugelvand of Pearson's Education Press for allowing me to draw upon some of the work I have done with Paul Graham in our *Introduction to Political Theory*. Gratitude needs also to be expressed to Bryan Turner, editor of the *Cambridge Dictionary of Sociology*, for permission to make use of some of my entries in this present volume.

Also those who refereed the project, had kind things to say, and Edinburgh University Press who are very efficient and thoughtful publishers to write for.

I would like to dedicate this book to the memory of Lisa Bloxham (the partner of James Hamill, a good friend of mine). Lisa died suddenly on 2 April 2005.

Introduction

This work assumes that politics cannot be studied without theory. All our statements about parties, movements, states and relationships between them presuppose theoretical views, so that political theory is an integral part of the study of politics.

Why then are students of politics so nervous about theory? One reason has to be that political theory has traditionally been presented in an abstract fashion. By this I don't mean that theory looks at concepts and movements in *general* terms. It is perfectly true that theory is not simply concerned, for example, with democracy in the UK in the 1990s, but with democracy as such. This generality can make students feel nervous and unanchored, but this problem can be (at least partly) offset by specific references and examples, and by the use of a language that avoids awkward terms – or carefully explains them where they are necessary.

What makes political theory *abstract* in the pejorative sense of the word is a remoteness from reality and what the ordinary person in the street thinks of as political controversies. A major cause of this kind of abstraction is the idea that there is an unbridgeable gulf between facts and values, the empirical and the normative. I see this as a dogma that either treats theory as an analysis of data (in the tradition that prevails in much of the writing by political scientists in the USA) or regards it as 'purely' normative so that theory is disdainful of the facts. Contrived examples are used instead of instances from history or contemporary controversies. All political statements combine the normative and the empirical, values and facts, and it is impossible in my view to say anything about politics that does not have an ethical implication. Even statements about individuals and freedom are controversial for those who espouse anti-liberal and fundamentalist views. The more that political ideas and theorists can be related to political realities (in the sense of everyday controversies), the more lively and interesting they become. Context is crucial and it needs to be continually spelt out.

This view of politics inevitably affects the choice of concepts and the theorists listed. The key factor underpinning my choice has been the theorists and concepts that I have found central to my own teaching. I have tried to bring the theorists to life by saying something about their background as well as their publications, and the concepts chosen, of course, express my own values and outlook. This is particularly true with concepts like the state, government, sovereignty and relationships. Where I have views that many reject, and the position adopted reflects my own particular eccentricity, I have tried to make this clear. I seek to explain both the traditional usage and why I depart from it.

I have found it useful to formulate the notion of a 'momentum concept' – an idea that captures both the continuity a concept has with the past as well as the need to reformulate it in the light of changing historical conditions. Thus, the concept of freedom is a momentum concept because it has a future rather different from its past. In ancient times, it was linked to the state; then under the influence of classical liberalism, it was defined as freedom from external interference. Today it needs to incorporate a positive dimension so that freedom involves *both* an absence of external interference *and* a capacity to do things. This, however, is not the end of the road. The idea of a momentum concept sees change as *infinite* since future generations will add to the notion of freedom, to continue our example, in ways that we cannot envisage today.

I passionately hold the view that introductory books do not need to be simplistic because they are introductory, or that a definition that is profound must for that reason be complex and elusive. I have sought to link the academically respectable with a lively and relevant presentation. How far I have succeeded I must leave to others to judge.

Where a word appears in **bold**, this indicates that it has its own listing within the glossary.

A Glossary of Political Theory

A

abstraction This involves a search for generalities. The word 'chair' abstracts 'chairness' from a large number of particular chairs so that we can identify it. However, when the term is used pejoratively, it implies more than this. Abstraction is a practical as well as a theoretical process, and means a search for similarities at the expense of differences.

All theory involves abstraction in that generalities enable particular entities to be identified despite their differences. Every word we use is abstract to an extent, since it is impossible, for example, to use 'table' (to take a rather well worn example) without 'abstracting' from the differences between real tables – some are brown, some are red, some are long, others short, and so on.

It is impossible to think without abstraction in this sense. Abstraction is not merely a theoretical process, but a practical one as well. **Marx** argues in *Capital* that 'abstract labour' relates to a real process of production in which the **power** and social position of the actors as well as their particular skills have been pushed to one side, so that all that is represented in the sale and purchase of commodities, is what workers and the work process has in common.

When used pejoratively, abstraction denotes a process that ignores relevant differences and therefore distorts reality as a result. The idea of the 'abstract individual' is problematic because the process of abstraction leaves out characteristics that are relevant to understanding their behaviour, for example whether such individuals are women rather than men; poor rather than rich; black rather than white, and so on. Used in this way the notion of abstraction is mystifying, since it expresses what people have in common at the expense of what differentiates them.

Further reading: Sayer 1987

agency A concept that denotes free will. Agents are people who can act.

Only with **liberalism** are all people assumed to be agents but it is important not to treat agency abstractly. Classical liberals, like **Hobbes** and **Locke**, assumed that agency was something that was innate in people and considered it to be 'god given' and **natural.**

In fact, agency has to develop as people enter into relations with one another, and acquire a sense of individuality and responsibility.

Agency can only be regarded concretely if it is linked to the existence of constraints. Agents need to recognise the existence of constraints, whether social or natural, in order to overcome them, and therefore agency, like **freedom,** can be seen as the creative recognition of necessity. Thus a free person is not the person who ignores obstacles, but the one who is able to surmount them.

Agents are contrasted to **structures**, and it is clear that both are necessary for a realistic analysis of human behaviour. Agency must be regarded as a **momentum concept**, that is, it is an attribute that we cannot finally realise, but need to work towards.

See also: **liberalism, natural, freedom, structure, momentum concept**

Further reading: Ball, T. 1978

alienation Denotes a process by which a person is dominated by a product they have created themselves. The key word in this process is *domination*. An alienated person or society is one in which their own creations appear strange or *alien* to them so that instead of taking control of their creations, they allow them to dominate them.

Marx developed the notion of alienation from his reading of Ludwig **Feuerbach** who had used the notion against religion, arguing that people worshipped a god of their own making. Marx applied the concept to money and capital, taking the view that people were controlled by, rather than exercised control over, society's wealth. He argued that worshipping the objects of one's creation was not simply an economic problem: it applied to social, political and cultural institutions as well. The **state**, for example, was an alienated institution since people were unable to see that the divisions making the state necessary were not **natural**, but had been created by humans, and could therefore change.

It is possible therefore to speak of thought processes themselves being alienated, where they assume that ideas exist that are beyond human control. Critics of the concept see the notion of an 'unalienated' society as vague and utopian.

See also: **Feuerbach, natural, utopianism**

Further reading: Fromm 1956

Althusser, Louis (1918–90) Born in 1918 in Algiers. He was active in Catholic youth organisations. Although he passed the entrance exam to the École Normale, he was interned in a prisoner of war camp in 1940 and here he spent the rest of war.

In 1948 he joined the Communist Party and since he had done well at the Ecole, he joined its staff. He became an advocate of structuralism, and *For Marx* appeared in 1965, followed by *Lenin and Philosophy* in 1969.

Althusser argued that **Marx** must be purged of all traces of **humanism** – the belief that humans can control their own destiny – and he stressed that Marx's theory must be seen as a science of bourgeois society. Marx's *Manuscripts of 1844* had been, he argued, inspired by **Feuerbach**, and because he was hostile to **Hegel**, Althusser took the view that Part I of *Capital* was misleading and unrepresentative. The notion of **alienation** was unMarxist because it implies a humanist emanicipation, and he insisted that there were two Marxes – a young Marx, who was a humanist, and an older Marx, a scientist, and they were separated by what Althusser called an 'epistemological break'. Marx, as he saw it, was not writing about capital as a material reality, but as an object of thought.

In *Lenin and Philosophy* he advances the view that we should characterise education and the media as ideological **state** apparatuses as opposed to repressive state apparatuses, and his critics have argued that such a characterisation fails to account for the relative independence of society from the state in a liberal society.

He was influenced by **Eurocommunism** and argued that classical **Marxism** was in deep crisis. He murdered his wife in 1980 and was confined to an asylum and released three years later.

See also: **humanism, Hegel, Feuerbach, Marx, alienation, Eurocommunism**

Further reading: Callinicos 1976

anarchism A theory that opposes all forms of rule over individuals. Anarchists are opposed both to the state and social pressures of all kinds.

Although many anarchists are socialists, not all are. Philosophical anarchists like **Godwin** were radical liberals who argued against the **state** on the grounds that it interfered with the supremacy of a person's private judgement. **Stirner** argued for an association of sovereign individuals, taking the view that all ideologies were oppressive because they eroded this individual sovereignty. Woolf, a contemporary philosophical anarchist, sees all individuals as autonomous although he accepts the case for direct democracy in a way that worries other anarchists, because this implies that individuals must be bound by majority rule.

Philosophical anarchists present their arguments in terms of abstract theory, whereas anarcho-capitalists, the most famous of whom is **Rothbard**, argue that the 'free market' if extended throughout society, can replace the state.

More conventional anarchists follow the arguments of the French theorist **Proudhon**, who opposed not only the state and **government**, but also all forms of collective workers' action like strikes. Rather more militant was the Russian anarchist **Bakunin** who saw the need for violent destruction, rooted in a human instinct for solidarity and revolt. Anarchists like the scholarly **Kropotkin** (also a Russian) argued that cooperation was vindicated by evolutionary processes, and he sternly took the Russian Bolsheviks to task for their authoritarianism.

Although some anarchists like **Tolstoy** rejected violence, it has been argued that because anarchists reject liberal forms of political organisation, they encourage their supporters to resort to bullets rather than ballots. The dogmatic rejection of religion that some anarchists espouse became a real problem during the Spanish civil war. The anarchists not only opposed the Republican government at war with Franco's nationalists, but they also burnt down churches in an attempt to rid society of all repressive hierarchies.

Anarchism remains an influential theory among those who feel that conventional **politics** has failed to improve society. Moreover, many **new social movements** (like peace, environmental and feminist movements) may support particular anarchist ideas without necessarily supporting the theory as a whole.

See also: **Godwin, Stirner, Rothbard, Proudhon, Bakunin, Kropotkin, Tolstoy, new social movements**
Further reading: Marshall 1993

animal rights An argument that seeks to go beyond the question of welfare for animals, and argues that animals must be placed on a par with humans in terms of their suffering.

The concept – and the movement that it has generated – takes the view that to allow humans to dominate animals is profoundly wrong, and singles out Descartes's characterisation as animals as mere machines for particular ridicule.

Bentham took the view that animals have the capacity to suffer, and animal rights advocates argue that while animals may not be able to speak or use reason, the fact that they can suffer makes them equal to humans.

The argument that humans are superior to animals is labelled as 'speciesism', a chauvinism akin to racism or sexism. Animals are sentient beings who should not be made to suffer through experimentation for human purposes, and should not be eaten.

Animal rights theorists differ as to whether the interests of animals are to be championed on utilitarian grounds (suffering destroys their happiness) or whether animals actually have rights, but in practice both sides agree about the need to grant animals the capacity to live their lives without human cruelty.

The theory suffers from a classical liberal view of **equality** as sameness. It is true that animals can suffer, but it does not follow from this that we should disregard the profound differences between animals and humans. Rights entail responsibilities, and just as animals cannot have duties, so it is hard to see how they can have rights either. The case for animal welfare is a compelling one, but it has to be said that animals exist ultimately for human development.

See also: **Bentham**

Further reading: Singer 1977

Arendt, Hannah (1906–75) Born in Hanover. She studied at the University of Heidelberg.

In 1929, Arendt completed her dissertation on the concept of love in Augustine. However, the rising anti-Semitism afflicting the German polity distracted her from metaphysics and compelled her to face the historical dilemma of German Jews.

When the National Socialists came to power, Arendt became a political activist. She escaped to Paris, where she remained for the rest of the decade. Working especially with Youth group Aliyah, Arendt helped rescue Jewish children from the Third Reich and bring them to Palestine.

When the Wehrmacht invaded France less than half a year later, she was interned. In May 1941, she managed to reach neutral America. In 1951 she published *The Origins of Totalitarianism*, where she traced the steps toward the distinctive twentieth-century tyrannies of Hitler and **Stalin**.

She wrote a good deal for Jewish journals, and was associated with *Partisan Review*. An expanded edition of *The Origins of Totalitarianism* was published in 1958, taking into account the Hungarian Revolution of two years earlier.

Arendt's next three books – *The Human Condition* (1958), *Between Past and Future* (1961), and *On Revolution* (1968) – sought to reconstruct political philosophy, and in 1963 she also published *Eichmann in Jerusalem*. Her portrayal of a bureaucrat who claimed to be following orders was strikingly original.

She was the first woman to become a full professor (of **politics**) at Princeton University, and she subsequently taught at the University of Chicago, Wesleyan University, and finally the New School for Social Research. She criticised military intervention in Vietnam, and in 1975 the

Danish **government** awarded Arendt its Sonning Prize for Contributions to European Civilization, which no American and no woman before her had received.

Further reading: Parekh 1981

Aristotle (384–22 BC) Born in Stagira in northern Greece. His father hoped that he would be a doctor.

In 367 he joined the academy of **Plato** in Athens where he remained for twenty years. After he left the academy, he travelled to Assoss, where he probably began work on *Politics* as well as a work *On Kingship* that is now lost.

In 343 BC he became a tutor to the young Alexander the Great (although this is disputed) but returned to Stagira, taking his group of philosophers and scientists. Alexander persuaded Aristotle to create a rival academy, which he founded in 335 BC in Athens. Here he is said to have lectured on a wide range of subjects including economics, meteorology and zoology.

On Alexander's death in 322 BC, anti-Macedonian feelings swept through Athens, forcing Aristotle to retreat to the family house in Chalcis, where he died a few months later.

Although his genius extended into a wide variety of subjects, he wrote much on political science. He examined the constitutions of the Greek city-states, but his most important work is *Politics* where he focuses on the **state** or *polis*.

He sees the **state** as **natural**, and his argument that 'man' is a political animal suggests that humans naturally live together in households, villages and states. The 'good life' can only be obtained in the state, and states need to be small and self-sufficient. Aristotle's **conservatism** can be seen from the fact that whereas he regards kingship, aristocracy and constitutional **government** as 'proper' forms, not only is tyranny and oligarchy a 'deviant' form, but so is **democracy**. He takes **slavery** and **patriarchy** for granted. His politics are authoritarian and his texts are important for an understanding of pre-liberal thought.

See also: **Plato, natural, democracy, slavery, patriarchy, state**

Further reading: Mulgan 1977

authority A contentious concept that some see as a form of **power** while others contrast it to power.

Authority involves a **relationship** between one individual or group and another, and is characterised by persuasive pressures rather than a threat of **force**. Authority is often linked to **morality** and **legitimacy**, but the problem with the latter link is, some argue, that legitimacy can be based upon an irrational support for an elitist leader (think of Hitler or **Stalin's** legitimacy), whereas authority requires a willingness to be critical.

The notion becomes a universal attribute under **liberalism**, which argues that influence can only be exercised where it has been authorised. Authority is linked to **consent,** but it is misleading to think that authority does not coexist with constraint. Clearly, when a patient recognises the authority of her doctor, she acknowledges the constraints she is under, and seeks help.

The authority of the **state,** it could be argued, is inherently problematic, since authority is undermined by force, and even individuals who are not the direct recipients of the force of state are aware of the presence of this force, and this influences their attitude towards state 'authority'. The term 'authoritarianism' that ought to be the opposite of authority captures the uncomfortable link between the 'authority' of the state, and erosion of free choice that the state implies.

See also: **power, force, morality, legitimacy, consent, liberalism, state**

Further reading: Carter 1976

autonomy An important concept that denotes self-government and independence.

The concept only acquires universal status with the rise of **liberalism**. However, because the term is treated in an abstract fashion, it ignores most of the population. It assumes that autonomous individuals are white, rational, **property**-owning, Christian men and hence excludes women, workers, artisans, blacks, and so on.

But the term helps to clarify the notion of **freedom** since autonomy implies a positive (and not simply a negative) view of liberty. An autonomous person has to have the resources to govern their own life.

Autonomy can only, it could be argued, exist in relational terms. It cannot imply an absence of constraint or restriction for these are inherent in **relationships**. It suggests that such constraints are recognised and transformed, so that governing your own life cannot occur in a vacuum. Autonomy is both an individual as well as a collective attribute: a person can only become autonomous if others are autonomous as well.

Moreover, the notion is a **momentum concept**. Autonomy is a situation we move towards, rather than actually reach: it is a progressive and not a static concept.

See also: **liberalism, freedom, relationship, momentum concept**

Further reading: Lindley 1986

B

Bakunin, Mikhail (1814–76) Born northwest of Moscow. At fifteen, he was sent to the Artillery School at St Petersburg. He was posted to a brigade in Poland but resigned from the army in 1836 in order to teach philosophy in Moscow.

Influenced by Fichte and **Hegel**, he went to Berlin in 1840 and joined the **Young Hegelians**. He travelled to Zurich where Weitling, a German communist, made a deep impact upon him. In Paris, he met **Marx** in 1844 but preferred **Proudhon**. Expelled from Paris under Russian pressure – he advocated the independence of Poland from Russia – he took part in the French **Revolution** of 1848 and wrote a fiery *Appeal to Slavs* in Prague in the same year. He participated in the insurrection in Dresden in 1849. Captured by Prussian troops, he was eventually deported to Russia and spent eight years in prison. When Alexander II became Tsar in 1855, Bakunin was banished to Siberia where he remained until 1861.

When he moved to Italy, he began to advocate social rather than national revolution, and developed his theory of **anarchism**. He established a secret revolutionary brotherhood, hierarchical and centralised, while calling for the destruction of the **state** and for the organisation of society by free association and federation. He joined the First International but in 1869 clashed with Marx who accused him of trying to set up an International within the International. He worked for a short time with Nechaev, a Russian nihilist, and in so doing damaged the reputation of anarchism. He was involved in the short-lived insurrection in Lyon.

He was enthusiastic about the Paris Commune of 1872 and wrote his first and last book, *The Knouto-German Empire and the Social Revolution*, between 1870 and 1872.

See also: **Hegel**, **Young Hegelians**, **Marx**, **Proudhon**, **state**

Further reading: Marshall 1993

Baudrillard, Jean (1929–) Born in Reims, France. He began his teaching career at the University of Nanterre and was an eager participant in the events in Paris of May 1968.

He published *The System of Objects* in 1968, followed by the *Society of Consumption* in 1970. In 1972 he wrote *A Critique of the Political Economy of the Sign*. The classical Marxist critique of political economy needed to be augmented, he argued, by semiological theories of the sign. What had proliferated was what Baudrillard called 'sign value' – the product of advertising, packaging, the media and the sale of commodities.

In 1973, his *Mirror of Production* attacked classical **Marxism** for its productivist bias, and in his *Symbolic Exchange and Death* in 1976, he argued that the logic of symbolic exchange must replace the capitalist logic of production. Modernity has come to an end, and we live in a 'hyperreality' in which images, spectacles and the play of signs predominate. Differences between individuals and groups dissolve, and images, codes and models mould individual identity.

He now described himself as a terrorist and nihilist in theory – his discourse drew heavily upon scientific metaphor, black holes, DNA, computer language, and so on. In *Simulacra and Simulations* (1981) he declared that the media are responsible for the way people behave, and in *Fatal Strategies*, published the following year, he contended that the endless proliferation of objects (their 'ecstasy') results in inertia, a complete saturation.

In the 1990s he published *The Transparency of Evil* and the *End of an Illusion* and he stirred up great controversy by arguing that the Gulf War never happened. As with 11 September 2001, it must be seen as a media spectacle.

Further reading: Kellner 1989

Bebel, August (1840–1913) Born near Cologne. He trained as a cabinet maker. In 1865 he attended the First German Women's Conference, held in Leipzig. In 1866 he joined the First International. In 1867 he founded the Saxon's People's Party and in 1868 he was elected to the North German parliament. The following year he helped to create the Social Democratic Workers Party which merged to create what was later called the Social Democratic Party (SDP).

In 1872 he was imprisoned for two years for treason as a result of his opposition to the Franco-Prussian war. From 1871 he was a member of the Reichstag, the German parliament, a position he held until his death.

In 1875 he published a book on the *Peasant War* and in 1879 he published his significant *Women and Socialism*. This book was widely read and helped to attract interest in Marxist ideas in Germany. The **emancipation** of women is, he argued, integral to the struggle against **capitalism**. Sexual activity between men and women is private, and people no longer attracted to one another should be able to freely separate. This work is considered by feminists today to be more sympathetic to the position of women than Engels' *Origin of the Family, Private Property and the State*.

In 1880 he met **Marx** and **Engels**, and contributed substantially to the party journal, *Neue Zeit*.

In 1891 he played an important part in creating the SDP's Erfurt Programme, and in 1903 he opposed the German **government**'s intervention in China, and argued passionately against protectionist measures in the economy. He debunked the view that education was somehow non-political. He published his autobiography in 1911.

See also: **Marx, Engels**
Further reading: Maehl 1980

behaviouralism A political theory – not to confused with *behaviourism* – that argues that we can only study events, that is, 'behaviour' rather than activity. Hence behav-iouralists see themselves as 'scientists' studying facts (that are presented as theoretical systems) rather than values. A theory of the cold war period, it became discredited in the late 1960s as a result of ethical dilemmas posed by the Vietnam War. This war compelled many academics to abandon the idea that political theory could simply side-step questions of value.

Further reading: Easton 1965

Bentham, Jeremy (1748–1832) He entered Queen's College, Oxford, at the age of twelve and was admitted to Lincoln's Inn at the age of fifteen.

In 1776 he wrote *A Fragment on Government* and in 1789 *Introduction to the Principles of Morals and Legislation* was published. Here Bentham argued famously that the proper objective of all conduct and legislation is 'the greatest happiness of the greatest number'. All acts are based on self-interest, it being the business of the law to ensure through painful sanctions that the individual subordinates his or her own happiness to that of the **community**. A plan for the reform of the French judicial system won him honorary citizenship of France.

In 1798 Bentham wrote *Principles of International Law*. He hoped that some form of European Parliament would enforce the liberty of the press, free trade, the abandonment of all colonies and a reduction in the money spent on armaments.

In 1809 he published *Catechism of Reformers* where he attacked the law of libel. His work was popularised by radical reformers and when Burdett argued the case for universal suffrage in the House of Commons in 1818, he quoted Bentham in his support.

In 1824 Bentham helped found the *Westminister Review*, the journal of the philosophical radicals.

His most detailed account of his ideas on political **democracy** appeared in his massive (and unfinished) *Constitutional Code*. Here he supported political reform, the abolition of the monarchy, the House of Lords and the established church. Women, as well as men, should be given the vote, while **government** officials should be selected by competitive examination.

Further reading: Parekh 1974

Berlin, Isaiah (1909–97) Born in Riga, Latvia. In 1921, he moved with his parents to London. He was educated at St Paul's School and at Corpus Christi College, Oxford.

Between 1932 and 1938 Berlin was a Fellow of All Souls College, where he studied philosophy and in 1939 his biography of Karl **Marx** was published. In 1938 he moved to New College, where he remained until 1950. During World War II he worked for British Information Services in New York and Washington, and in 1945, he spent three months in Moscow and Leningrad.

He published widely on music and philosophy but increasingly turned his attention to the history of ideas. In 1953 he published *The Hedgehog and the Fox: An Essay on Tolstoy's View of History*. His lecture on historical inevitability was delivered in 1954, and in 1957 he became Chichele Professor of Social and Political Theory at All Souls College. He was knighted that same year. His inaugural lecture on *Two Concepts of Liberty* argued the case for a negative concept of **freedom** (freedom from) that he distinguished from positive freedom (freedom to). His argument has sparked a debate that continues to this day. From 1949 he regularly lectured in the United States, and in 1966 Berlin accepted the Presidency of Wolfson College. In 1969 he published his *Four Essays on Liberty*.

He retired from the University in 1975 but had already become President of the British Academy, a position he retained until 1978. In 1976 he published a book on Vico and Herder. Berlin lived to see the publication of numerous uncollected and unpublished writings through the efforts of his editor, Henry Hardy.

Berlin was a Governor of the Hebrew University of Jerusalem. He had a lifelong passion for music, and became a Director of the Royal Opera House, Covent Garden.

See also: **freedom**

Further reading: Gray, J. 1996

Bernstein, Eduard (1850–1932) Born in Berlin. Bernstein worked as a bank clerk before he joined the Social Democratic Party (SDP) in 1872. The party enjoyed increasing electoral success, and as a result Bismark passed an anti-socialist law that drove Bernstein into exile. He eventually moved to Britain where he worked closely with **Engels** and members of the **Fabian** Society.

While living in London, Bernstein became convinced that the best way to obtain socialism in an industrialised country was through trade union activity and parliamentary **politics**. He published a series of articles in which he argued that the predictions made by **Marx** about the development of **capitalism** had not come true. The real wages of workers were rising and the polarisation between an oppressed proletariat and exploiting capitalist **class** had not materialised. Nor had capital become concentrated in fewer hands.

Bernstein's 'revisionist' views appeared in his extremely influential book *Evolutionary Socialism* (1899). His analysis of modern capitalism challenged the argument that **Marxism** was a science and upset the orthodox. Socialists like **Bebel, Kautsky,** Liebkenckt and **Luxemburg** still believed that a Marxist **revolution** was possible.

Although he led the right wing of the party in the Reichstag, the German parliament, he eventually opposed his country's participation in the First World War. He helped to form the Independent Socialist Party in 1917, and he was hostile to the Russian Revolution. Elected to Reichstag in 1920, he fiercely condemned the Nazis.

See also: **Engels, Fabianism, Marx, Bebel, Kautsky, Luxemburg**

Further reading: Gay 1962

Bookchin, Murray (1921–) Born in New York, he entered the Communist youth movement in the 1930s. After the Stalin–Hitler pact of September 1939, he was formally expelled from the Young Communist League for 'Trotskyist-anarchist deviations'.

Bookchin participated in the great General Motors strike of 1946, but he began to question traditional Marxist ideas about the 'hegemonic' role of the industrial proletariat. In the late 1940s and early 1950s, Bookchin wrote agitational literature that opposed not only nuclear weapons but also the peaceful uses of the atom, because of radioactive fallout. In 1956, he demanded US intervention on behalf of the uprising in Hungary against the Soviet Union.

He started publishing articles on ecological issues. *Ecology and Revolutionary Thought* (1964) argues for a political marriage of **anarchism** and **ecology**, while *Towards a Liberatory Technology* (1965) asserts that alternative technologies could provide people with the free time necessary to engage in civic self-management and a democratic body politic.

Bookchin's essays from the 1960s have been anthologised in *Post-Scarcity Anarchism*. In the late 1960s he taught at the Alternative University in New York, and later at City University of New York. In 1974 he co-founded the Institute for Social Ecology and became its director; in the same year he began teaching at Ramapo College of New Jersey.

Bookchin has also written extensively on urban issues. He is currently working on a three-volume history of popular movements in the classical **revolutions**, called *The Third Revolution*.

Further reading: Biehl 1997

Bull, Hedley (1932–85) Born in Sydney, where he studied at the University. He went to Oxford University in 1953. He became a lecturer in international relations at the London School of Economics in 1955.

He travelled to the USA in 1957, but was critical of **behaviouralism**. (He wrote a lively defence of the classical approach to international relations in 1966.) In 1961 he published *The Control of the Arms Race*. In 1965 he became the director of the Arms Control and Disarmament Research Unit based in London and established by the Foreign Office, and two years later, he accepted the post of Professor at the Research School of Pacific Studies at the Australian National University in Canberra. He travelled widely, spending a year at the Jawaharal Nehru University in India. During this period, he edited a book on *Asia and the Western Pacific*.

In 1977 he accepted a chair at Oxford, and in the same year he published what is undoubtedly his major work, *The Anarchical Society: A Study of Order in World Politics*. Here he argues that the international order is a society, governed by law and **common interests**, even though there is no world **state** overarching it. He raises a number of fascinating questions. He rejects the Hobbesian version of the international system as too narrow, the Kantian view as too 'idealistic' and argues in favour of the Dutch jurist, Grotius. Ultimately, he argues, order has to prevail over **justice**.

In the numerous articles he wrote after this book, he viewed the third world sympathetically, and in 1984 published *Justice in International Relations*.

See also: **behaviouralism**

Further reading: Miller and Vincent 1990

Burke, Edmund (1729–97) Born and educated in Dublin. Burke moved to London, published *A Vindication of Natural Society* in 1756, and *A Philosophical Enquiry into the Origin of Our Ideas of the Sublime and the Beautiful* a year later.

He became interested in **politics**, and served as the Lord Lieutenant of Ireland between 1761 and 1764. In 1765 he was appointed private secretary to the Prime Minister, Lord Rockingham, and was a spokesperson for the Rockingham Whigs (that is, liberals), publishing among other pamphlets his *Thoughts on the Causes of the Present Discontents* in 1770.

From this time until 1787 he acted as an agent for the British parliament in the colony (as it was then) of New York but he failed to persuade parliament to meet American demands. It was as an MP for Bristol that he made his famous plea for representatives to act independently, and from 1784 to 1794 he represented Malton, a borough that the Rockinghams controlled.

Between 1782 and 1783 he was Paymaster General, urging that Warren Hastings be impeached for his misdemeanours in the East India Company that then ruled India. He astonished his Whig supporters by fiercely criticising the French **Revolution** in his best known book, *Reflections on the Revolution in France* that was published in 1790. This became a classic of **conservatism** with its defence of tradition, gradualism, and prejudice, and he contrasted the English constitution of 1688 and

the French upheaval of 1789 that he considered dangerous and abstract.

Burke came to be regarded as the founder of conservatism because of his dislike of abstract ideas and his
defence of 'prejudice' – that is to say, ideas that are rooted
in custom, tradition and 'instinct'.

Further reading: Macpherson 1982

C

capitalism Although definitions differ according to ideological tradition, there is a general agreement that capitalism is based upon a **market** in which labour itself is
bought and sold.

The Marxist view sees capitalism as a system in which
the capacity of the worker – labour power – is bought and
sold as a commodity. The exchange process is regarded by
Marx as a mysterious process in which the labour that
gives commodities value is rendered abstract – that is, its
particular properties are concealed. When labour power is
bought and sold, the particular circumstances of the
worker and capitalist are hidden so that it appears that a
fair exchange takes place. Marx argues that the worker is
necessarily exploited since he or she receives a wage that is
equivalent (under conditions of perfect competition) to the
value of their labour power – what it takes to reproduce
them as workers. Since there is a difference between the
value of their labour power and the amount they produce,
surplus value is generated that enriches the capitalist.

Feminist critics of Marx have argued that labour
as the source of value is often interpreted in a way that
ignores value that is produced by workers (usually
women) in the home. More traditional critics have
argued that value also depends upon risk-taking and

those who invest capital are entitled to receive dividends as a result.

Although capitalism is praised (even by Marxists) as a dynamic system, socialists and (even social liberals) worry about the inequalities and violence that it generates. The wealthy live longer, are more healthy and enjoy life more: capitalism is seen by its critics as a divisive system that creates victims as well as beneficiaries.

See also: **Marx**

Further reading: Sanders 1995

church (also religion) An institution that ritualises and organises religious belief. Not all religions have churches: it is possible to believe in a spiritual creator without belonging to a particular church.

It could be argued that it is wrong to assume that people are religious by nature. Early peoples practised magic in which they commanded nature to act, rather than religion in which nature or spiritual forces are worshipped.

Religion is of the utmost importance in understanding politics and the state. Ancient Greeks, for example, believed in multiple gods who had obvious human strengths and weaknesses, but with the rise of monotheism, it is believed that a single god creates the world. In the medieval world, access to this god was confined to the few and some believed that holy texts were the word of god, written in a particular language that only the learned could understand. This explicitly hierarchical system reached its apex in a ruler who was seen as god's vicar on earth. With the Reformation however, in Europe, individuals could communicate directly with their creator, and the holy text was written in the vernacular. There is clearly a link between Protestantism historically and the rise of **liberalism**.

Most political theorists see a connection between religion and the state, although confusingly liberals argue that the church and state should be separate. Yet it is plausible to suggest that there is clearly link between unquestioning obedience towards your creator and obedience to the state. **Rousseau** believed that the link was so important that he would have had atheists put to death. Critics of the state are often hostile to churches in particular, on the grounds that they deflect attention away from social problems that people confront in their daily lives.

See also: **politics, state, liberalism, Rousseau**

Further reading: Tawney 1969

Chomsky, Noam (1929–) Born in Philadelphia. His undergraduate and graduate years were spent at the University of Pennsylvania where he received his Ph.D. in linguistics in 1955. During the years 1951 to 1955, Chomsky was a Junior Fellow of the Harvard University Society of Fellows. While a Junior Fellow he completed his doctoral dissertation on 'Transformational Analysis'. The major arguments of the dissertation appeared in *Syntactic Structure* (1957). This formed part of a more extensive work, *The Logical Structure of Linguistic Theory*, which was published in 1975.

Chomsky joined the staff of the Massachusetts Institute of Technology in 1955 and in 1961 was appointed full professor in the Department of Modern Languages and Linguistics. From 1966 to 1976 he held the Ferrari P. Ward Professorship of Modern Languages and Linguistics.

In 1958–9 Chomsky was in residence at the Institute for Advanced Study at Princeton, and in the following years he delivered a number of key memorial lectures. He has received honorary degrees from many universities. He is a Fellow of the American Academy of Arts and

Sciences and the National Academy of Science, and has received a number of honours both for his contribution to linguistic theory and his work for peace.

He has visited many countries in South America, the Middle East and Asia, arguing passionately that the USA has caused destruction and misery in its foreign policy. He is particularly concerned with the way in which the media in the USA and Western Europe projects what he sees as a superficial and misleading view of US policy, and he seeks in his campaigning work and writing to develop a radical critique of these policies.

Further reading: Lyons 1970

citizenship An old notion that has traditionally been linked to a person's right to participate in the affairs of the state. Recently, however, it has become a subject of intense interest.

Citizenship in ancient Greece and Rome was restricted to free men who were Greek or Roman. Although **liberalism** spoke expansively of the **rights** of individuals, women and the propertyless were excluded from political rights, and it is only in the twentieth century that citizenship becomes universal in a formal sense.

Marshall in his classic work on *Citizenship and Class* argued that in Britain, civil rights were won in the eighteenth century, political rights in the nineteenth, and in the twentieth century, citizenship involved the granting of social rights resulting from the welfare state. Critics have complained that this ignores the particular position of women, and it could be argued that women are still 'second class' citizens in Britain today.

Theorists have also become more sensitive to the different ways in which citizenship in different countries has been formally attained; the part that ethnic, religious and

class difference plays in enabling people to exercise the rights of citizenship; the problem posed by the state as an institution claiming a monopoly of legitimate **force**, and the question of whether citizenship can and should be global, rather than national in character.

The somewhat negative view of citizenship, fashionable in the 1960s and 1970s with writers under Marxist influence, has given way to an explosion of concern about the nature of citizenship, and debates about the **market, equality, nation** and the state are often conducted around the concept of citizenship.

See also: **liberalism, Marshall, state, class, market, equality, nation**

Further reading: Faulks 2000

class An important category, class is a political as well as economic term. It denotes not simply a person's economic **power**, but what kind of political influence they can exert.

Elitists like **Pareto** and **Mosca** argue that every society is governed by a ruling class, by which is meant a minority who are able to perpetuate their domination through superior organisational skills and psychological attributes.

The term is often used to assign people a particular status depending upon their income, but Marxists use the term to denote the relationship a person has to the means of production. A class analysis would then involve say a study of political events in terms of actors who occupy differential positions in relation to the ownership of capital.

The use of the concept of class has been marginalised recently by the idea that class is merely one identity among many, and people can see themselves in ethnic, regional, gender or sexual terms rather than as people who are rich or poor. A challenge would be to define the concept of class so that it underpins these other identities – class would only express itself in daily life through these other identities. This would at least avoid the somewhat mechanistic juxtaposition of class as a separate factor that exists alongside gender, ethnicity, and so on.

See also: **Pareto, Mosca**
Further reading: Wright 1985

coercion This involves the use of pressure amounting to a threat of credible **force**. Coercion is not the same as force, since it is a threat to use **force**. On the other hand, this threat has to be credible or coercion cannot be said to exist.

The term is sometimes employed to describe social pressures that compel people to work for others or to conform to a moral climate of public opinion. **Marx** speaks of the market as coercive even for those who own **property**, and J. S. **Mill** speaks of the moral coercion of public opinion. Here is a broad view of coercion that relates to circumstances in which no credible force is threatened.

It is better to refer to these kinds of pressures as constraints, and to use the term coercion to refer to the threat of credible force. Coercion cannot exist without force, even though it is not synonymous with it.

See also: **force, Marx, Mill**
Further reading: Hoffman 1995

Collingwood, R(obin) G(eorge) (1889–1943) Born in Lancashire. He became a fellow of Pembroke College in 1912, and Professor of Metaphysical Philosophy in 1935.

In his *Speculum Mentis*, which he published in 1926, he sees art, religion, science, history and philosophy as an ascending order of knowledge – each building on its successor. In his *Essay on Philosophical Method* in 1933 he presents this as a dialectical process stressing that history, rather than nature, influences philosophy. All thought rests upon presuppositions, and when a 'bedrock' is reached, we have absolute presuppositions that cannot be verified by experience. In *The Idea of Nature* he challenged the **positivist** view of natural science, arguing that scientific propositions depend upon historical conditions.

In 1946 he published his *Idea of History*. All history, he asserted, is a history of thought. Influenced by the **idealism** of the Italian philosopher **Croce**, Collingwood saw a crucial distinction between human activity and the events of nature. In order to understand an act, one must try to get inside a person's head and understand their thoughts.

In 1937 he published *The Principles of Art* and in 1939 his *Autobiography* where he urged the philosopher to adopt a 'gloves off' approach and not shrink from political practice. The *Essay on Metaphysics* further elaborated his philosophical arguments, and in 1942 he produced *The New Leviathan* that urged that self-respect should be consciously cultivated by **government** and education. Western civilisation sought to develop according to an ideal, but as Nazism showed, could return to a period of barbarism that resembled a Hobbesian state of nature. Here he wrestled with the problem of relativism: can one assert that the absolute presupposition underlying a liberal civilised society is superior to the absolute presupposition that underlies barbaric Nazism?

See also: **positivism**, **Croce**
Further reading: Bouchier 1994

common interest This is an important concept because when a common interest exists, it is possible to resolve **conflict** without violence or **coercion**.

Of course we are assuming that common interests

extend across as well within **communities**; otherwise a common interest may simply unite one group against others, as in times of war.

Common interests do not exclude the existence of disagreements and conflict but they imply that the parties to a dispute have sufficient in common to 'change places' and thus resolve their dispute through negotiation, arbitration or compromise.

See also: **community, conflict**
Further reading: Bull 1977

communism A system in which the production of goods and services is communally owned. Communism can imply a society without **classes** and the **state**, although Plato's notion of communism was clearly statist. It has been argued most notably by **Engels** that early tribal societies were communistic.

Communism has been espoused by some anarchists as well as Marxists. Both see communist societies as stateless and classless although anarchists would exclude **government** and constraint from communism, whereas Marxists arguably would not.

Marxists have generally described communism as a phase that follows on from socialism, and none of the Communist Party states described themselves as communist in character, even though they were called 'communist' by their opponents.

The construction of modern communism involves the transcendence of **capitalism** and the **market**, and it is hard to see communism emerging except as a global system. According to **Marx**, communism is the beginning of a new kind of **history**: it is not, as so often thought, the end of the historical process.

See also: **class, state, Engels, history**
Further reading: Tucker 1978

communitarianism A theory that became influential in the 1990s and sought to place the **community** at the heart of political theorising.

Communitarians express strong opposition towards the abstract individual of liberal theory, arguing that people need to participate in running their lives. They view with alarm the tendency to retreat from political and social involvement into privatised worlds in which people act simply as consumers.

Communitarians are aware that elevating the community may generate a regime that imprisons rather than empowers the individual. Order and autonomy, they contend, should nourish one another, so that individuals become more able to govern their own lives when consciously participating in communities.

It is important to see communities, they argue, in the plural. A community is a 'set of attributes', Etzioni argues, not a place, so that people should be committed to numerous communities, each with their norms and culture. The more individuals are monopolised by any one community, the less 'communitarian' such a society will be.

Each community is deemed part of a wider community, so that values cannot be restricted to one particular group, but must be linked to global values – values that express the interest of the community of communities.

The problem with many expositions of communitarianism is that they see the need for a 'balance' between order and autonomy. This means that they adopt statist attitudes towards the provision of order, and liberal attitudes towards autonomy, taking the view that we should not have too much of either. This view leaves intact the very institutions that in practice (it could be argued) challenge the reality of communities. Communitarians could only address this criticism by working out a strategy (however long term) for moving beyond both **market** and **state**.

See also: **community, market, state**

Further reading: Etzioni 1996

community This has become an important and fashionable concept over recent years, particularly with rise of **communitarianism**.

The emphasis upon the individual, characteristic of **liberalism**, has given way to a recognition that people belong to communities. There is however a danger of privileging one community over others, since this expresses a community identity at the expense of an individual's right to choose. **Marx** described the **state** as an 'illusory community' on the grounds that it presented its partisan **interests** in spuriously universalistic terms, and it is clear that unless a person sees themselves as belonging to numerous communities (as most communitarians acknowledge), there is a danger that the notion of community will imprison rather than liberate the individual.

This would require that the notion of community is defined in a way that respects and builds upon the liberal tradition rather than suppresses it.

See also: **comunitarianism, liberalism, Marx**

Further reading: Taylor 1982

conflict A clash of wills that conventionally is seen as involving violence or the threat of violence.

Obviously conflict can take this form, but it could be argued that conflicts of interest arise in all social **relationships** so that we could distinguish between conflict that involves **force** and **coercion**, and conflict that can be resolved through social pressures that involve neither.

Politics could then be defined in terms of conflicts that are resolved and no use of force is involved. Where conflicts involve force, then inevitably the **state** or states are involved.

See also: **force, coercion, politics**

Further reading: Hoffman 2004

consent An act of affirmation to a rule or law or indeed to any proposed course of action.

Essential to the notion of **authority**, the concept becomes a universal attribute of human relations with **liberalism**. All acts of authority must be subject to consent from those who accept them, but the problem with liberal formulations, it could be argued, is that they are abstract. Theoretically, the problem of constraint is pushed aside so that the real social pressures that cause a person to consent in a particular way are ignored.

It follows from this argument that the problem of consenting to acts of **force** by the **state** is an insoluble problem for liberal theory, and the statement by Jean-Jacques **Rousseau** that 'the murderer consents to die' can only be sustained if people are given an imaginary pure 'will' that co-exists alongside their real one.

Consent is crucial to a **democracy**, but the concept has to be linked to a recognition and transformation of constraints. It cannot exist in some kind of vacuum.

See also: **authority, liberalism, democracy**

Further reading: Pateman 1985

conservatism Although the term is occasionally used to define a disposition or attitude to life, conservatism is best understood as an **ideology** and a political movement.

It is argued – particularly by conservatives who follow the ideas of **Burke** – that conservatism is too flexible to be an ideology or be an 'ism'. But conservatism certainly has a set of principles. Conservatism sees people as naturally unequal, and conservatives argue that the notion of **difference** expresses itself in the form of **natural** hierarchies – between men and women, 'civilised' and 'uncivilised', and so on. Conservatives, for this reason, have at times opposed **democracy**, sexual **rights** (that is, relations between gays and straights) and gender **equality**, the rights of all nations to determine their own destiny, and so on. Conservatism is not just a philosophy of 'realism'. Conservatives may advocate radical change in egalitarian societies that they deem 'unnatural'. The status quo only deserves to be conserved if it is conservative!

Conservatives favour the concept of family, **state**, religion and nation. The family is seen as de-emphasising individual choice, while charity is preferred by some conservatives to welfare rights since the former relies upon the benevolence of the few rather than the entitlements of the many. Private **property** is supported but the **market** must not undermine tradition and **hierarchy**.

The state is favoured as an institution since some conservatives argue that people need leaders and authorities to tell them what to do and think. Religion is important since conservatives are sceptical that people can act in an orderly way without an element of prejudice and mysticism.

Historically, conservatism supported empire, and while the conservatives of one nation will differ from those of another nation, mutual antagonism arises from broadly shared principles.

See also: **Burke, difference, natural, equality, market, hierarchy, state**

Further reading: Willets 1992

corporatism This refers to organised interest groups that mediate between society and the **state**.

In fascist theory, corporatism is seen as a substitute for **democracy** so that major groups are 'licensed' by the state to exercise control over 'their' section of the population.

In the post-war period, corporatism is not restricted to business corporations, but often includes the larger trade unions as well. A limited number of relatively privileged groups play a role in determining public policy in consultation with the state. This contradicts the assumptions of liberal theory. Individuals are not all equal, and the role played in the determination of policy by a relatively small number of actors is unrecognised in the democratic process.

Unlike the notion of interest-group **pluralism**, corporatism assumes that relatively few organisations of a non-competitive kind relate to the state in a privileged way. A distinction is sometimes made between 'societal corporatism' where powerful groups in society – usually employer and employee associations – are recognised by the state, and 'state corporatism' where the state itself takes the initiative and imposes a scheme upon dominant groups. The latter is usually associated with more authoritarian state systems.

Corporatism is defended as a way of imposing order upon society, so that the **market** itself is controlled and inflation and unemployment managed. In Britain the **government** of **Thatcher** sought to eliminate corporatism, arguing that corporatism was a kind of feudal and hierarchical system that privileged the producer over the consumer.

However it would naïve indeed to imagine that free-market societies do not have 'pockets' of corporatism, whether in terms of powerful agricultural **interests**, or leading capitalist sectors that ensure that the state responds positively to their bidding.

See also: **Thatcher**

Further reading: Cawson 1986

Croce, Benedetto (1866–1952) Born in the Abruzzi, southern Italy. He studied law at the university in Rome.

He rejected **Marx**'s determinism, insisting that art must be a product of free expression. In 1900 he published *Historical Materialism and the Economics of Karl Marx* in which he was critical of Marx's analysis of **capitalism**.

In 1902 he published *Aesthetic*. Encouraged by Gentile to read **Hegel**, he wrote *What is Living and What is Dead in the Philosophy of Hegel* in 1907. He published three volumes on philosophy, the *Philosophy of Spirit*, the *Philosophy of Practice* and in 1911 *The Philosophy of Giambattista Vico*. He saw philosophy as a kind of secular religion: theory was oriented to the spiritual sphere of the Beautiful and the True while practice aimed at the Useful and the Good. There are no transcendent or objective standards since each 'moment' derives from the historical process. He strongly endorsed **Hegel**'s motto: 'what is real is rational; what is rational is real'.

In 1910 he became a senator and served as Minister of Education under Giolitti between 1920 and 1921. In 1915 he published the *Theory and History of Historiography*. He was intensely hostile to socialism and initially welcomed the fascist seizure of **power**. However, he became increasingly critical of the fascist regime, and in 1925 issued a protest against intellectuals like Gentile who saw in **fascism** the unity of theory and practice. He wrote a number of historical works that argued for the importance of 'ethico-political' moment in civilisation. His best known is probably *History as the Story of Liberty*, published in 1938.

He was a minister without portfolio in 1944 and published his *Studies on Hegel* in 1952.

See also: **Marx, Hegel**

Further reading: Croce 1946

Crosland, Anthony (1918–77) Educated at Highgate School and Trinity College, Oxford.

He saw war service in Italy, and in 1946 he graduated in **politics**, philosophy and economics at Oxford. He became a lecturer at Trinity until 1950 when he was elected as a Labour member of parliament, first for Gloucester (1950–5) and then for Grimsby (1959–77).

In 1953 he published *Britain's Economic Problem* and three years later, his best known book, *The Future of Socialism*. Here he argued that **Marxism** had become irrelevant, as **capitalism** had been transformed through democratic pressures, and the trade unions had become powerful political actors. Ownership was less important than managerial control: there was a welfare state, full employment, low inflation and continuous growth. Socialism was linked to **equality**, and equality was more efficient, socially unifying and just.

Between 1956 and 1958 he was secretary of the Independent Commission of the Cooperative Movement and from 1958 to 1963 he was a member of the Consumer's Council. In 1961 he brought out *The Conservative Enemy*. Crosland served as a Minister of State for Economic Affairs in 1964–5 and was Secretary of State for Education up to 1967. He was involved with local **government** and planning until 1970, and between 1974 and 1976, he was Secretary of State for the Environment.

In 1974 he published *Socialism Now* – a work that makes use of **Rawls'** *Theory of Justice*. Not only would comprehensive education help to break down **class** barriers, in his view, but he also saw economic growth as making it possible to improve the position of the worst off, while allowing those who were better off to preserve their living standards. He became Foreign Secretary in 1976.

See also: **equality, Rawls**

Further reading: Crosland 1982

D

Dahl, Robert (1915–) Born in Iowa, and has taught most of his life at Yale University.

Although Dahl is best known for his numerous works on democratic theory, he published *Congress and Foreign Policy* in 1950, *Domestic Control of Atomic Energy* in 1951 and *Politics, Economics and Welfare* in 1952. His concern with **democracy** and his argument that democracy involves the conciliation of numerous minorities was aired in *Preface to Democratic Theory* in 1956.

In 1961 he published the book for which he is probably most famous, and which began a prolonged debate around the question of **power** – *Who Governs?* He was concerned to integrate the question of democracy into a wider theory of politics. In 1963 he published a book that has gone into many editions, *Modern Political Analysis*.

A concern with oppositions was published in 1966, and following the 1968 student rebellions, Dahl published in 1970 a work entitled, *After the Revolution*.

He taught in Chile in 1967 and his growing reputation was reflected in the fact that he became president of the American Political Science Association in 1966–7. Further works on democracy followed in 1972 and 1973, but Dahl was becoming increasingly concerned by a problem that had not appeared to worry him earlier – the political power of corporate wealth. In *A Preface to Economic Democracy* in 1985 he addressed the way in which concentrated wealth can impact on the liberal democratic system, and in the same year he returned to the subject of nuclear weaponry. Further books on democracy followed, with a work in 1994 revealingly entitled *The New American (Dis)Order*.

Dahl has received many honorary doctorates and won many prizes for his work.

See also: **democracy, power**
Further reading: Dahl 1961

democracy A confusing concept. Since the Second World War, it has become obligatory for all politicians, with the exception of fundamentalists, to describe their **states** as democratic, no matter how authoritarian they are. Democracy means rule of the people. A liberal polity in which all adults are entitled to vote is a necessary condition for democracy. But it could be argued that for a democracy to prevail, inequality has to be tempered so that conflicts of interest can be settled through compromise and negotiation.

It is useful to examine the **relationship** between democracy and **liberalism**, since liberals historically opposed democracy on the grounds that it was a system that favoured the poor and subverted the **market**. The founding fathers of the US Constitution are better described as liberal republicans rather than democrats, and although **Tocqueville** called his classic work *Democracy in America* (1835–40), it was an analysis of a liberal rather than a democratic culture.

Conservatives were fond of branding their liberal opponents democrats, on the grounds that liberal principles had egalitarian implications. Yet early liberals supported **property** rather than universal political **rights**, and it was only in the mid-nineteenth century that liberals like James **Mill** and **Bentham** began to make a cautious case for universal suffrage.

Although new liberals like Hobhouse appeared to be supporters of democracy, they agonised over support for **imperialism** and wanted restrained legislatures. A favourite liberal argument against democracy is that the system leads to a 'tyranny of the majority', and even after the Second World War, some political theorists favoured low popular participation, warning of the authoritarian proclivities of the 'masses'.

These problems arise because democracy is seen as a form of the state, whereas it could be argued that there is a tension between the notion of democracy as self-government and an institution – the state – claiming a monopoly of legitimate **force** for a particular territory. It is now argued by some that democracy is a global concept and must embrace international institutions.

See also: **liberalism, Tocqueville, Mill, James, Bentham, state**

Further reading: Held 1987

Derrida, Jacques (1930–2004) Born in El-Biar, near Algiers.

In 1948 he enrolled in the philosophy class at the Lycée Gauthier in Algiers, and was greatly influenced by Kierkegaard and **Heidegger**. In 1950 he went to France, and at the Ecole Normale Supérieure, he worked with Hyppolite and **Althusser**. His Masters thesis was on Husserl, and he spent 1956–7 studying at Harvard.

He did his military service in Algeria, returning to France in 1959. In 1960 he moved to the Sorbonne, and in 1962 he published a translation of Husserl. Three years later he joined the staff of the Ecole Normale Supérieure, and became linked to the journal *Tel Quel*.

In 1967 he published *Speech and Phenomena*, *Of Grammatology* and *Writing and Difference*, returning to Algeria in 1971. The following year he published *Positions*, *Dissemination* and *Margins of Philosophy*. He taught regularly at Johns Hopkins and Yale Universities in the US. In 1974 he published *Glas*, a work that examined the convergence of literature and philosophy. In 1975 he became involved with a pressure group to tackle **government** proposals in the teaching of philosophy and in 1976, *Of Grammatology* appeared, translated by Gayatri Spivak.

He has published on **Nietzsche**, writing *Deconstruction and Criticism*. In 1981 he was arrested in Prague for running 'clandestine seminars'. The French government intervened to secure his release. In 1983 he helped with an International College of Philosophy that sought to make tuition available to non-academics. His concern with deconstruction attracted widespread interest.

In 1987 he became a Visiting Professor at the University of California, Irvine. He published a stream of books, receiving (despite intense opposition) an honorary degree at Cambridge University in 1992. In 1994 he published *Spectres of Marx*.

See also: **Heidegger**
Further reading: Wolfreys 1998

determinism A concept generally used negatively by political theorists to denote a dogmatic closure of thought. Determinism is seen as fatalism, a belief that particular activities are pre-ordained and unconditionally inevitable.

This is true of the determinism linked to the liberal tradition. This tradition postulates a dualistic coupling of free will *or* determinism, so that determinism is seen as a mechanistic kind of necessity – an event that has to happen.

But determinism does not have to be treated in this dualistic fashion, and it could well be argued that a mechanistic determinism requires some kind of 'god within the machine': in order to explain how people are active, the postulate of free will has to be introduced. A consistent determinism can simply be taken as a belief that everything is caused and therefore 'determined', however complex this causality is. Thus a determinist can accept that great individuals make an impact on history, because they play a part in the wider canvas of events. But unless one holds that causes are not at work in the real world, then it is impossible not to be a determinist in practice, whatever position is held in theory.

Further reading: Hoffman 1975

dialectical materialism The philosophical basis of Marxist theory. There is controversy as to whether dialectical materialism was created by **Engels** or **Lenin** rather than **Marx**. Although it was later to be presented very schematically, the theory itself underpins Marx's analysis of society, history and the world itself.

Dialectics can be taken to refer to the fluidity of all things – their movement and change – and it is a concept that locates this change within things. A dialectical view of **capitalism** points to the fact that capitalism grew out of an earlier system and must itself change. This change is seen as 'eternal', in other words something that must always occur.

Hegel's theory sees dialectical change as the development of mind, and it could be argued that this theory unwittingly breaks with dialectics insofar as it is based upon unfolding ideals, and this **idealism** postulates a beginning and an end.

Engels presented dialectics in terms of 'principles' like the unity of opposites and the transformation of quantity into quality. When water boils, for example, increasing heat (a quantitative change) transforms the water into steam so that a change in quality occurs. Although it was Engels who put forward these views, there is some evidence to suggest that Marx did not dissent from this. A dialectical approach sees everything as contradictory. Things pull against one another: they are inherently unstable and must change.

Materialism is a theory that postulates that the material world exists independently of consciousness. It is a theory of knowledge – valid ideas are those that reflect this independent reality accurately – as well as a theory of being or **ontology**. The brain is 'matter that thinks' so that even the most fantastic ideas are produced by people thinking in the real world. Even prejudiced ideas (like racism, for example) arise as reflections of material reality, even though these reflections are superficial and one-sided.

Materialism is an old theory but it can only be sustained logically if it is dialectical. The notion of a beginning or an end is both undialectical and non-materialist since it necessarily implies the existence of an idealist creator of some kind.

See also: **Engels, Lenin, Marx, dialectics, idealism**
Further reading: Engels 1964

dialectics Initially assumed to be a method of reasoning, linked to formal logic. A dialectical approach involved raising questions as in **Plato**'s dialogues so as to expose contradictions within an opponent's position. This would have the effect of making the coherent and defensible answer irresistible.

Dialectics features prominently in **Hegel** where dialectical processes denote change and development in the world itself. Hegel's exposition of dialectics as the unity of opposites, the negation of the negation and the transformation of quantity into quality applied to nature as well as society. What causes the world to change and develop? It is, for Hegel, the presence of 'spirit' – a god who is in everything – and this raises the problem of how such a spirit is created and dies. By making dialectics a principle of the Divine Idea, it could be argued that Hegel contradicts his own principles since a creator who creates itself and cannot die is an undialectical construct.

Marx claimed to have inverted Hegel's dialectical method, thus creating what came to be called **dialectical materialism**. Although this question is controversial, dialectics for Marx is, it could be argued, both a **natural** and a social process, since the development of distinctively human characteristics becomes unintelligible unless they are the product of a dialectical nature. Marx does not see dialectics as necessarily antagonistic (if by this is meant violently oppositional) although dialectical processes in **class**-divided societies will involve violent **conflict**. The contention is that communism is not the end of history, but itself a dialectical society based upon the tension between the forces and relations of production. Critics have warned that the general exposition of dialectics is a philosophical task that cannot produce any real knowledge: only the sciences, natural and social, can do this.

See also: **Plato, Hegel, Marx, dialectical materialism**
Further reading: Norman and Sayers 1980

difference An important concept that is intended to recognise diversity. This concept has only been focussed on with the development of **feminism** and **multi-culturalism**.

Everyone has an identity but this identity is unique and thus different from every other. Every woman, like every man, is different from others, in terms of her age, wealth, language, religion, and so on.

But the notion of difference becomes divisive unless it is linked to sameness. One without the other either leads to a suffocating and oppressive uniformity or to a chasmic divide that creates enmity. Difference is **natural** and an attribute to celebrate rather than arouse alarm.

This is why it is crucial to be able to distinguish between real differences and imaginary ones. The fact that people have different skin colours (a real difference) does not mean that white people are more intelligent than black (an imaginary 'difference'). The problem with some postmodernists is that they interpret difference in a way that obliterates this distinction and therefore it becomes impossible to use the term difference in an empowering and democratic way.

Further reading: Hughes 2002

division   A **conflict** between parties – whether they are individuals or groups – that cannot be resolved without the use of **force**. It is not simply that there is a distinction involved: it is that the people or groups cannot change places or empathise with the other's position. Hence when divisions occur, **states** are directly or indirectly involved, since in these circumstances a conflict cannot be addressed through negotiation, arbitration or compromise.

Further reading: Hoffman 2004

Dworkin, Andrea (1946–2005) Born in Camden, New Jersey, and educated at Bennington College. Dworkin worked as a waitress, a receptionist and a factory worker before becoming involved in the women's movement.

In 1980 she published *Take Back the Night: Women on Pornography* and a year later, *Pornography: Men Possessing Women*. She was involved with **MacKinnon** in an unsuccessful campaign to secure the passage of an anti-pornography ordinance that would have allowed aggrieved persons to sue those who had produced, sold or distributed 'offensive' material. She sees pornography as a form of violence against women, and regards it as perpetuating the domination of women and their hatred by men.

She championed a radical **feminism** that has become unfashionable but she was a vigorous defender of the dignity and autonomy of women.

She wrote *Right-Wing Women* (1983), *Ice and Fire* (1986), *Letters from a War Zone 1976–1987* (1989) and a work entitled *Mercy* in 1990.

See also: **MacKinnon**

Further reading: Dworkin and MacKinnon 1988

E

Easton, David (1917–) Born in Toronto. Educated at Toronto and Harvard Universities and taught at the University of Chicago.

In 1949 he published a critique of liberal **realism**. Easton's growing interest in, and sympathy for, what he was later to call the 'behavioural **revolution** in political science' is evident in his work on the 'democratic elitist' Harold Lasswell.

In 1953 he published his work *The Political System*. Here he argued passionately against the **state** as the 'orienting' concept for political science, and contended that **politics** is much better defined in terms of a system that 'authoritatively allocated values for society as a whole'. This definition made it possible to locate politics in all societies, including stateless ones.

From 1957 to 1958 Easton was a member of the Centre for the Advanced Study of the Behavioural Sciences, and served on a variety of important academic boards. In 1957 he began to flesh out his model in an article for *World Politics* and in the 1960s he coupled his interest in **behaviouralism** with detailed analyses of the attitude of young people towards the American political system.

In 1965 he argued for the merits of behaviouralism in a work entitled *A Framework for Political Analysis* and then provided a lengthy and detailed analysis of his system in *A Systems Analysis of Political Life*. In these works he sought to refine his analysis by introducing the concept of 'persistence through change', arguing that a system could change its regime and institutions profoundly, and yet still persist.

In 1968–9 he was president of the American Political Science Association and in 1981 he returned to the question of the state, publishing his *Analysis of Political Structure* in 1990.

See also: **state, politics, behaviouralism**

Further reading: Easton 1971

ecology A concern with the **politics** of the environment.

The ecological movement is diverse, and addresses issues like the treatment of animals, the use of resources, the need to explore alternative forms of energy and technology, the quality of food that is consumed, the problem of pollution, and the negative impact that humans have on the world of nature.

Environmentalism has become a major **new social movement**, often concerned with direct action, and suspicious of conventional politics. The view is generally taken that official responses to the environmental crisis are woefully inadequate, and some ecologists see a tension between the health of the environment and a belief in the market economy.

The movement not only challenges the vision of endless and irresponsible consumption, but sees the importance of unintended consequences in analysing the problem of environmental degradation. Some elements link environmentalism to **feminism**, arguing that violence towards nature is an extension of violence towards women.

The movement divides over whether concern for the environment is linked to the well-being of humans, or whether the earth represents a system in its own right.

Ecocentrics argue that many Greens are concerned with prioritising human rights, and ignore the **rights** and needs of nature as a world in itself.

Environmentalists see the ecological question in global terms and are acutely aware that inequalities between north and south make it more difficult to resolve environmental problems.

A concern with the environment has massive implications for traditional political theory, and it is certainly true that normalising violence between humans is linked to a dismissive and elitist view of the environment. Nature is the inorganic body of humans, and it is difficult to see how humans can develop, if the wider world of nature is treated with contempt and manipulation.

See also: **new social movements**

Further reading: Porritt 1984

elitism The term denotes a minority that dominates society and has a monopoly of **power**.

It is particularly associated with **Mosca** and **Pareto** who argued that all societies, whether they are called monarchies, aristocracies or democracies, are ruled by an elite. The basis for elite rule varied. It could be economic, but it could also be symbolic, religious, military prowess, or, a factor particularly stressed by Pareto, psychological. The point is that even in a liberal **democracy**, it is an illusion to imagine that the people rule.

Elite rule is generally ascribed to a combination of **coercion** and **consent**. While brute force is used, it is skilfully blended with cunning, and the coordination of members of the elite gives them superiority over the 'mass'. In **Michels'** argument, particular emphasis is placed upon organisational skill. Elites are able to perpetuate themselves not only through flexibility, but also the cooption of those from 'below' who show initiative.

Although the elitists claimed to be disinterested scientists, it is clear that the target of their argument was social democracy and especially **Marxism**. Against the latter they insisted that wealth was simply one of many bases for elite rule, and the idea of a self-governing society was simply a myth.

This elitism was modified after the Second World War and became a theory of liberal democracy in which elites competed, thus giving a relatively passive population a 'choice'. Sometimes called 'democratic elitism', this view argued that the apathy of the bulk of the population was 'functional'. There could a plurality of **interests** but ultimately the key decisions were taken by relatively few.

See also: **Mosca, Pareto, Michels**
Further reading: Parry 1969

emancipation A term that means self-government either by an individual or by a group.

Initially the concept was associated with **liberalism** and refers to civil and political **rights**. Thus the emancipation of **slavery** meant that former slaves could exercise legal and political rights, and the emancipation of women resulted in the fact that the latter could own **property**, vote and stand for election.

The term has aroused criticism from some postmodernists who argue that the term suggests a universal notion of freedom and thus rides roughshod over local identities. Anarchists have also criticised the term, seeing it as a purely liberal concept.

However, it could be argued that governing your own life involves more than legal and political rights. It requires material resources – a reasonably paying job, shelter, health care, adequate education, and so on, so that in liberal societies, people are only partially emancipated.

Emancipation is a good example of a **momentum concept** in that it is a state of being towards which we need to move, but never actually reach. It would be misleading to say that in a particular society all its inhabitants are fully emancipated since we are always discovering new barriers that get in the way of emancipation.

See also: **liberalism, momentum concept**

Further reading: Laclau 1966

empiricism Empiricism is a philosophical position that seeks to confine study to the facts.

Formulated historically by **Hume**, empiricism identifies normative or ethical propositions as metaphysical or imaginary in character. Empiricists believe that factual statements are free from values, and that general principles are useful to have but they can never be proven.

Empiricism has been hugely influential, particularly in the English-speaking world. It was linked particularly in the 1950s and 1990s with a notion that the study of **politics** could only be 'scientific' if it stuck to the facts and saw ethical propositions as purely personal and private protestations of faith.

Empiricism, its critics argue, rests upon an untenable dualism between facts and values, theory and practice, and ignores the way in which facts are inherently evaluative since they are related to one another, and it is this **relationship** that furnishes the evaluative implications. Thus, the proposition that fewer and fewer people vote in a liberal **democracy** because they are satisfied with politicians may be presented as a purely factual statement (and indeed, was so presented by political scientists in the 1950s and 1960s), but it has obvious normative implications.

See also: **behaviouralism, Hume**

Further reading: Bruce 1970

Engels, Frederick (1820–95) Born in Barmen, Germany. At the age of 16, Engels went to work for the family firm. He first met Karl **Marx** in 1842 and in 1844 the two agreed to work together.

The Condition of the Working Class in England is acknowledged as Engels' masterpiece. He and Marx joined the Communist League and Engels penned the draft upon which Marx based *The Communist Manifesto.* After the suppression of the 1848 revolutions, Engels moved with Marx to Britain, writing articles under Marx's name for the *New York Daily Tribune.* He also produced *The Peasant War in Germany* and *Revolution and Counter-Revolution in Germany.*

He retired in 1869, and moved to London. Here he wrote *Anti-Dühring.* In 1894 he published *Origin of the Family, Private Property and the State* and, four years later, *Ludwig Feuerbach and the End of German Classical Philosophy.* His *Dialectics of Nature* was published posthumously in 1927.

After Marx's death, Engels devoted the rest of his life to editing and translating Marx's writings.

See also: **class, communism, history, Marx, state**
Further reading: McLellan 1977

equality A political concept that implies that people with similar attributes need to be treated in the same way.

The pre-liberal tradition defended equality in a way that excluded most of the population. Citizens were equal, but divided naturally from slaves or serfs.

The liberal tradition extends equality to all human beings, but this equality, it could be argued, is abstract and ignores the differences between people. To meet this argument, equality needs to be defined in a way that makes it compatible with **difference** so that to treat people equally, is to acknowledge and respect their difference.

In what respects therefore are people equal? They are all human and all have the capacity to develop. Equality is a concept that recognises this and it must have consequences for the distribution of resources. Inequality of a radical kind prevents people from 'changing places', and therefore is a cause of force and frustration.

Equality is a **momentum concept** since it is unimaginable that a 'truly equal' society can be realised. What we can and should do is to make our society more equal, and extend the notion from humans to the wider world of nature, where we need to recognise commonalities as well as difference.

See also: **difference, momentum concept**

Further reading: Pennock and Chapman 1976

Eurocommunism A trend within the communist movement that became influential in Western Europe in the middle of the 1970s.

It argued that orthodox communists, particularly those in Eastern Europe, had ignored the democratic content of Marx's thought, and Eurocommunists took the view that a communist society can only result as an extension of **democracy**, either conceived in parliamentary terms, or through extra-parliamentary pressures.

Eurocommunists argued that the concept of the dictatorship of the proletariat, like the theory of **dialectical materialism**, was dogmatic and authoritarian. They turned to **Gramsci** in particular for a view of **Marxism** that emphasised the importance of **morality**, and respect for the liberal tradition.

See also: **Gramsci**

Further reading: Claudin 1978

F

Fabianism The doctrine of a society formed in Britain in 1884, and named after the Roman consul, Fabius, who was famed for his gradualist and step-by-step tactics.

The Fabians rejected **Marxism**, and argued for a form of socialism that would emphasise the importance of training experts in public affairs; stress the need for rational argument and the advocacy of reform (as opposed to **revolution**), and support parliamentary **democracy**. Fabians see socialism not as an overall way of life, but in terms of specific projects based upon hard-headed factual information.

The Fabian Society still exists and produces pamphlets on the reform of foreign policy, the civil service, the national health service, the case for and against the adoption in Britain of the euro-currency, and so on.

It is a constituent part of the Labour Party and remains hugely influential today.

See also: **Marxism**

Further reading: Cole 1961

fascism One of the major ideologies and political movements of the twentieth century. The term is sometimes used exclusively to describe Mussolini's movement in Italy but its scope is wider than this.

Fascism arises in situations in which liberal **democracy** appears to have failed, and whereas **Marxism** criticises **liberalism** from the 'left', fascism attacks from the 'right'. It is hostile to the notion of reason and individuality as a universal attribute. It regards the Enlightenment as espousing decadence and identifies with the collectivity rather than the individual, exalting **nationalism** and rejecting cosmopolitanism.

Fascism embraces modern technology and sees the **state** as the supreme expression, along with the nation, of personal loyalty. It is strongly opposed to notions of democracy, and identifies repressive **hierarchy** as **natural** and inevitable. It is intolerant of political oppositions and favours **totalitarianism**, and thus the rejection of all liberal freedoms.

Although German Nazism differed from Italian fascism in its hatred of Jews, fascism in general privileges a particular ethnic group. Fascism therefore always espouses some kind of racist doctrine.

Its attitude towards **capitalism** is ambiguous. It is hostile to liberalism and the free **market**, but in practice fascists can come to terms with capitalist **interests**, even though they subject the latter to nationalist and statist regulation.

Although fascism was a major movement in the interwar period, it continues in the post-war period, rejecting immigration, and expressing visceral opposition to pluralist respect for different cultures. The British National Party and the French National Front are examples of current fascist parties.

See also: **liberalism, nationalism, state, natural, totalitarianism, capitalism, market**

Further reading: Nolte 1969

Fanon, Frantz (1925–61) Born in Martinique, but in 1947 he went to France to study medicine and psychiatry.

In 1953 he went to work as a psychotherapist in Blida-Joinville, Algeria, and became a supporter of the Algerian Liberation Front (FLN). In 1957 he resigned his position at the hospital in Algeria, having already published five years earlier *Black Skin, White Masks* (translated into English in 1970). He moved to Tunisia, and as part of his commitment to the FLN, edited supporting journals. In 1959 he wrote a book about the Algerian **Revolution**, and is particularly famous for his *Wretched of the Earth*, translated in 1965 and with a preface from **Sartre**.

In this book Fanon vehemently denounces colonialism, and appears to regard violence as personally and politically liberating. He argued for the revolutionary role of the lumpen proletariat (that is, the unemployed and criminals) and the rural masses, and stressed the need for third-world economies to socialise their resources and democratise their institutions.

His work on the African Revolution was published posthumously.

See also: **Sartre**

Further reading: Caute 1970

feminism Feminism is concerned with the **emancipation** of women.

It is so diverse that some prefer the term 'feminisms' to capture the multiplicity of the movement.

Feminism can be differentiated along ideological and philosophical lines. *Liberal* feminism seeks to expand the liberal concept of the individual so that women are included. This is the oldest form of feminism and historically has concentrated upon obtaining political and legal **rights**. *Socialist* feminism refers to the view that women are members of a particular **class** and suffer particularly under **capitalism**. *Radical* feminism argues that feminism stands or fall as a movement independent of other ideologies. Radical feminists see male domination as a personal as well as a wider institutional problem. It is men, and not simply class or autocracy, that are the barrier to women's liberation.

'Philosophical' feminism takes the form first of *feminist empiricism*, which stresses the importance of a sophisticated 'scientific' approach that emphasises the presentation of factual information to establish discrimination. *Standpoint theory* sees women as having a specific social experience that gives them particular insights into social problems that men cannot have, while *postmodern feminism* emphasises the problematic character of women as a homogenous category. Postmodern feminism argues that women are not only different from men, they are also different from one another. They are divided by class, ethnicity, religion, language and so on – indeed so much so that some postmodern feminists actually put the entire feminist project in jeopardy by arguing that women do not exist!

All feminisms contribute to the theory that women are equal to men and should be free to govern themselves, and it would be wrong to think that one particular variant has all the answers.

See also: **emancipation, capitalism**

Further reading: Bryson 1999

Feuerbach, Ludwig (1804–72) Born in Landshut in Germany and educated at Berlin under **Hegel**.

He soon became critical of Hegelianism and Christianity and in *Thoughts on Death and Immortality* published in 1830, he criticised theories of eternal life. In *A History of Modern Science from Bacon to Spinoza* (1833) he attacked dogmatism, and argued that nature needed to be rehabilitated against idealist philosophy.

In his *Essence of Christianity* (1841) he presented a naturalistic critique of Hegel, avoiding the term materialism because it was associated with hedonism. His argument was that 'the secret of theology is anthropology'. Religion is the mystified consciousness of humans so that when people worship God, they are merely worshipping an idealised version of themselves. People are religious because they are divided against themselves: 'Man asserts in God what he denies in himself'. Religion makes solidarity with others impossible because the values of earthly life are seen as unworthy and inferior. Religion is thus an **alienation** – a spectre that humans have created, and which dominates their life.

This book had a huge impact in Germany and beyond, and it enabled **Marx** to overcome Hegelian categories in his own thinking. Feuerbach's influence is particularly acute in Marx's writing in the first half of the 1840s.

In 1843 Feuerbach wrote *Principles of the Philosophy of the Future* in which he still cast his theory in Hegelian terms. In his *Lectures on the Essence of Religion* (1851), he defended an eighteenth-century materialism that denies the centrality of human activity in shaping the world. Egoism becomes part of human nature, and religion was now seen as a product of fear and ignorance. Humans were simply natural beings whose propensity to cooperate was derailed by religious fantasy.

See also: **Hegel, alienation, Marx**
Further reading: Wartofsky 1977

force Force arises where pressures are exerted in which a person ceases to be a subject, and becomes an object or thing.

The **state** uses force to tackle conflicts of interest, and it could be argued that it is impossible to resolve **conflicts** through the use of force: it is only possible to manage or suppress them.

The liberal tradition juxtaposes force with **freedom**, while defending the permanent need for a state. It is true that liberal states seek to limit force and restrict it to forms that are explicitly authorised, but it is arguable that force always goes to 'extremes' and the idea that force can avoid arbitrariness is fanciful.

A free society has to be one in which the use of force is no longer required and people can resolve their conflicts of interest through social and moral sanctions that do not require force.

The concept of force is sometimes extended to account

for all pressures that cause a person to do something that they had not intended. It is however best to restrict the use of force to the infliction of physical harm, understanding the latter to include psychological pressures that result in harmful consequences to a person's health.

See also: **state**

Further reading: Nicholson 1984

Foucault, Michel (1926–84) Born in Poitiers, France. In 1946 he was admitted to the Ecole Normale Supérieure.

From 1954 to 1958 he taught French in Sweden. In 1960, the year he returned to France as the head of the Philosophy Department at the University of Clermont-Ferrard, he published *Madness and Civilization*.

Foucault's second major work, *The Order of Things*, appeared in 1966. In this work he declared that 'man' was merely a discursive formation made possible by fundamental changes in the arrangement of knowledge during the last 150 years, and was nearing his end. Just as **Nietzsche** had proclaimed the death of God, so Foucault proclaimed the death of 'Man'.

Between 1966 and 1968, Foucault taught in Tunisia, returning to Paris to head the Department of Philosophy at the University of Paris. He was greatly affected by the student revolt of 1968.

Archaeology of Knowledge appeared in 1969. In 1970 he was elected to the College de France, the country's most eminent institution of research and learning, as Professor of the History of Systems of Thought. In 1975 he published *Discipline and Punish*, perhaps his most influential book. Here he saw the modern prison as a field of practice in which the human sciences and their techniques of normalisation were first developed, before testing them out on society as a whole. Truth and **power**, he now argued, operate interdependently.

During the last decade of his life he devoted himself to *The History of Sexuality*, a monumental but unfinished project. In the first volume, he sees the **state** as an institution that uses its knowledge and practices of the human sciences to construct the identity of its subjects. The second and third volumes came out shortly before his death.

See also: **state, power**
Further reading: Sheridan 1980

fraternity A **relationship** between individuals and groups that is akin to the relationship between siblings.

The notion arises from the bonds felt originally in a tribe. As a political term, this relationship involves a sense of cooperation in seeking to control one's own life. In ancient Greek thought, fraternity was deemed to exist between citizens. It was a particularly exclusive term, relating to men who were free and resident. However, unlike family bonds, fraternity implies choice: one freely selects one's 'brothers'.

In medieval Christianity, the term applies to all 'men' since all are equal in the eyes of their creator. However, not only is the notion explicitly patriarchal, but it is restricted to Christians, and it is mediated by rank, so that only those of the same 'station' can be deemed 'brothers'.

With the development of **liberalism**, the notion becomes more inclusive, and is tied to notion of **freedom** and **equality**. In practice, however, it could be argued that the term is still exclusive. It is linked members of a particular **class**, who are male, of a favoured religion and ethnicity, and so on.

Under the impact of **globalisation** the term has, however, developed a more inclusive scope. Feminists have, however, complained that the notion has a built-in male bias and it is inappropriate in a world aspiring to gender equality. But fraternity can be defined as a concept that includes all, men and women, and it emphasises the importance of developing **common interests** if people are to settle their differences without the use of **force**.

See also: **liberalism, freedom, equality, globalisation, class, common interests, force**

Further reading: Ignatieff 1985

freedom To be free is to be unrestricted. Freedom arises as a concept that applies to all with the liberal tradition.

Before the development of **liberalism**, only particular individuals were deemed free as in the distinction between 'freemen' and slaves. Classical liberalism argues that all are 'naturally' free, but in practice freedom did not extend to women, colonialised subjects, the propertyless, and religious minorities.

It has been argued since the Second World War that we need to distinguish between *negative* and *positive* freedom. The former involves 'freedom from' and is directed against deliberate interventions from other people. The latter is a 'freedom to' and involves the capacity of people to develop themselves.

The distinction is however problematic. A person can hardly be able to develop themselves if they are externally constrained, and having resources and capacities is little use if a person is prevented from making use of them. Freedom is therefore both negative and positive, and it could be argued that the classical liberal tradition assumed that the kind of individuals whom the theory addressed (white, male **property** owners) could take the question of capacity for granted. The distinction is developed as a reaction to new liberalism and socialism – ideologies that stress that without resources, freedom becomes formal and hypocritical.

Freedom is both a **momentum concept** and deals with individuals in **relationship** with others. It could be argued therefore that unless everyone is free, then no-one is free.

See also: **liberalism, momentum concept**

Further reading: Gray, T. 1990

Freud, Sigmund (1856–1939) Born in Freiberg in Moravia. In 1859 the family moved to Leipzig and then to Vienna.

Here he set up a practice in neuropsychiatry. He published *Studies in Hysteria*, jointly with Breuer in 1895. In 1900 he published *The Interpretation of Dreams*, and this was followed in 1901 by *The Psychopathology of Everyday Life*. In 1905 he wrote *Three Essays on the Theory of Sexuality*. His emphasis upon sexuality was highly controversial and it took some years before the importance of his work was recognised.

In 1916 he published *Five Lectures on Psycho-Analysis*. His work in 1923, *The Ego and the Id*, sought to analyse the mind in terms of the id, ego and super ego. The id is unconscious, irrational and amoral. Opposing this 'pleasure principle' is the 'reality principle' of the ego that seeks self-preservation. The home of repression and conscience – the source of 'civilisation' – is the super ego that seeks to transform the child into a social being.

In *The Future of an Illusion* (1927) and *Civilization and its Discontents* (1930) he argued that happiness has been exchanged for security, and Freud antagonised feminists by suggesting that women represent the **interests** of the family and sexuality, and are the foes of civilization. He was sceptical that socialism could work since, as he saw it, private **property** and war are the product of an inherent aggressiveness within human nature.

In 1939 the Nazi *Anschluss* with Austria forced him into exile in Britain.

Further reading: Roazen 1968

G

Gandhi, Mahatma (1869–1948) Born in Porbander, India. Following university, Gandhi went to London to train as a barrister. In 1891 went to South Africa.

Here he experienced racial discrimination, and developed his *satyagraha* ('devotion to truth') as a strategy of non-violent protest.

He returned to India in 1915 and by 1920 he had transformed the Congress Party. He launched the Non-Cooperation Movement that involved boycotting British goods and institutions. Large numbers were arrested and in 1922 he was sentenced to six years imprisonment. He was released after two.

In 1930 Gandhi sought to challenge the caste system and called the untouchables *harijans* (children of god). In the same year he established the Civil Disobedience Movement and one year later attended a Conference in London as representative of the Congress party. In 1934, however, he resigned from Congress.

He favoured the formation of self-sufficient villages and emphasised the need for developing crafts and settling disputes through arbitration rather than formally constituted law courts. He saw the **state** as representing violence in a concentrated form.

The Quit India Movement was established in 1942, and in 1947 Britain announced Indian independence, granting dominion status to both India and Pakistan. Gandhi was heartbroken by the divisions between Hindus and Muslims that led to partition. Appeals for calm were ignored and it was a Hindu fanatic who assassinated him in 1948.

Gandhi saw each person as divinely created and argued that the body should be fulfilled but not indulged, since spirituality is the source of our **morality** and true being.

He saw private **property** as an institution that worked against the 'oneness' of humanity, and he argued that the rich should be closely controlled by the state.

See also: **state**

Further reading: Iyer 1973

Giddens, Anthony (1938–) Born in London, Giddens received a BA from Hull University in 1959, and an MA and Ph.D. in 1974.

In 1961 he taught social pyschology at the University of Leicester. Here he met Norbert Elias, a sociologist with an international reputation, moving to the USA in 1969 and creating a faculty of Social and Political Sciences at the University of Cambridge. He was promoted to professor in 1987.

In 1971 he published *Capitalism and Modern Social Theory* and five years later, *New Rules of Sociological Method*. In *Central Problems in Social Theory* (1979) and *The Constitution of Society* (1984) he sought to develop his theory of structuration – a theory that attempts to give weight both to the question of **structure** and of **agency** in understanding society.

He helped to found Polity Press in 1985, and in 1997 he became director of the London School of Economics, a position he held until 2003. He was a member of the Advisory Council for the Institute for Public Policy Research and adviser to the British Prime Minister, Tony Blair.

He has been increasingly preoccupied with the question of **globalisation** (he delivered the BBC's Reith Lectures on the latter in 2000). In the 1990s he published a stream of books dealing with the question of modernity, personal **relationships,** and the '**third way**' – an attempt to renew social **democracy** in a manner that moves beyond the traditional positions of 'left' and 'right'.

In June 2004 he became a Labour member of the House of Lords.

Further reading: Tucker 1998

globalisation Not a purely economic phenomenon, but a political and cultural one as well. Globalisation, although rooted in the internationalisation of the **market** in the past, is a recent development and represents the 'shrinkage' of the globe as a result of trading, technology (in particular the computer **revolution**) and cultural exchange.

Right-wing commentators have seen globalisation as the spread of **capitalism** throughout the world, but this is better described as a pseudo-globalisation that works to accelerate inequalities both between countries and within them. It creates not a sense of global identity, but a fundamentalism that seeks either to restore an imaginary past in a violent and divisive way or to extol the present order as though it represents the culmination of history. Pseudo-globalisation creates conditions for terror, statism, war and repression.

It could be argued that globalisation, properly so-called, involves a concern with social **justice**, a search for global solutions to global problems and the promotion of economic **relationships** that are concerned with developing the poor and undeveloped regions of the world. Politically such globalisation would spread democratisation, so that people have growing confidence in their ability to influence policy-makers. As a global process, democratisation points to the impotence of the sovereign **state**, and urges people to think of themselves not merely as citizens of a particular country, but as 'citizens of the world'. **Common interests** come increasingly to the fore, whether it is a concern with beating back environmental degradation, combating poverty, or tackling divisive chauvinisms that marginalise women, minorities, so and on.

Culturally, globalisation requires a sensitivity to **difference,** an awareness that different ways of life enhance the world, just as the diversity of natural species should be preserved and protected. Globalisation seeks to strengthen what is developmental and weaken what is divisive and degrading.

See also: **difference**

Further reading: Stiglitz 2002

Godwin, William (1756–1836) The son of a poor Presbyterian minister, Godwin was influenced by Dissenters and became a Presbyterian Minister himself in 1768. He did not make a success of this and decided to earn his living from writing.

Although this was precarious, he got his publisher to finance him and he produced his major work, *An Enquiry Concerning Political Justice.* This was first published in 1793 and substantially revised for a second (1795) and third edition (1797). In 1794 he wrote his most successful novel, *Caleb Williams,* and three years later he married **Wollstonecraft** who died in childbirth some five months after their marriage. His *Memoirs* lost him public support and although he continued to write, he lived his final thirty years in debt and relative obscurity.

He espoused a theory of **anarchism,** based on a belief that individuals were rational and social beings whose autonomy was necessarily corrupted by **government.** A representative assembly was only permissible as a transitional expedient.

The capacity of individuals to judge is sacrosanct, and as perfectible beings, they can only progress through knowledge, truth and understanding. Many commentators find his anarchism implausible and concentrate on his **utilitarianism,** which they see as making an important contribution to the history of political thought.

See also: **Wollstonecraft**
Further reading: Marshall 1984

Goldman, Emma (1869–1940) Born in Lithuania. After six months in school, she had to work in a factory. She was sent to the US in 1869, after her father had tried in vain to marry her off. She was greatly influenced by the hangings that followed the Haymarket Square tragedy in Chicago in 1886 when a bomb was thrown into the ranks of the police during a workers' rally. She decided to become an anarchist.

With Berkman, she planned the assassination of Finch, a brutal employer who had suppressed strikes in the Homestead Pennsylvania factory. Finch was injured and although Goldman was not imprisoned, her lectures were regularly disrupted by the authorities. In 1893 she was imprisoned for a year.

She helped to edit *Mother and Earth* and in 1910 wrote *Anarchism and Other Essays*. *The Social Significance of Modern Drama* followed in 1914. She was imprisoned a second time for distributing birth-control literature, and again for her staunch opposition to the First World War. In 1917 she received two years for seeking to obstruct the draft, and after this, she was stripped of her citizenship and deported to Russia.

She supported the Bolsheviks but broke with the regime when the sailors and soldiers at Kronstadt were crushed by the Red Army in 1921. She left Russia that year and in 1923 she wrote *My Disillusionment in Russia*, followed a year later by *My Further Disillusionment in Russia*. In France she published her autobiography.

She went to Spain in 1936 to support the anarchists, where she was unhappy with their participation in the Republican **government**. She helped to establish a committee to aid homeless Spanish women and children.

Further reading: Drinnon 1970

government A concept that is often used as a synonym for the **state**. Where government is differentiated from the state, it is usually taken to describe the executive and elected branch of the state, as when one refers to the 'Labour Government'.

However the term has a broader and different usage, when it is taken to refer to the implementation of policies that seek order and regularity. The term 'governance' is sometimes used to capture this process, although the term government is useful because it can be used to account for regulation at a multiplicity of different levels.

An ordered individual is often referred to as a person who governs him or herself. All kinds of voluntary institutions in society – with greater or lesser degrees of formality – are also seen as having governments. It could be argued that governments in this context rely upon social pressures to secure the adherence to rules, and therefore are contrasted with the state, which uses **force** to secure order. In this use of the term, government seeks to resolve conflicts of interest through negotiation and compromise so that stateless societies, whether domestic or international, can be said to have government.

See also: **state, force**

Further reading: Hoffman 1995

Gramsci, Antonio (1891–1937) Born in Sardinia. As a child he was constantly ill, and his anguish was compounded by physical deformity. He won a scholarship to the University of Turin, and by 1913 he had become a socialist.

He was deeply influenced by the liberal **idealism** of **Croce**, and by 1915 he was writing regularly for the socialist *Cry of* *the People* and *Forward*, and stressing the importance of preparing the workers culturally for revolution. Following a four-day insurrection in August 1917 he became a leader of the Turin workers movement, and welcomed the Russian Revolution in Crocean style as a 'Revolution Against *Das Kapital*'. He helped to found *The New Order*, a paper that saw the factory committees in Turin as the nuclei of a future socialist state. The paper was also critical of the passivity and reformism of the socialist party, and Gramsci became a member of the central committee of the newly formed Communist Party of Italy. He was his party's representative in Moscow on the Third International.

In October 1922, Mussolini seized power: the head of the Communist Party was arrested and Gramsci found himself party leader. He was elected parliamentary deputy in 1924 but arrested two years later. He was sentenced to prison for twenty years, and although he started work on his famous *Prison Notebooks* in 1929, by the middle of 1932 his health was deteriorating rapidly and by 1935 he was too ill to work.

His notebooks were smuggled to Moscow and they are undoubtedly his masterpiece. They contain sharply perceptive analyses of Italian history, Marxist philosophy, political strategy, literature, linguistics and theatre. His emphasis upon the moral and intellectual element in politics offers a challenge not only to Marxists, but also to all seeking radical change in the world.

See also: Croce, politics

Further reading: Femia 1981

Green, T(homas) H(ill) (1836–82) Green was educated at Rugby and went to Balliol College, Oxford. He was deeply religious. He was a great admirer of the liberal politician John Bright (who was a passionate and famous advocate of free trade).

He translated Bauer's *History of the Christian Church* and was influenced by German philosophy and the romantic Carlyle (but strongly disapproved of the latter's racist views on blacks). He supported the Italian nationalist Mazzini, and the north in the civil war in the USA.

He was appointed to a Royal Commission on Education in 1864. He became a tutor and later Master of Balliol College. In 1867 he helped to get compulsory attendance at chapel scrapped for students, and was a strong supporter of electoral reform. In *Political Philosophy and its Relation to Life*, published in 1868, he makes it clear that while he admires **Hegel**, he regards **idealism** as ultimately subjective. He was defeated in the elections to the town council in 1874, and in 1881 published his *Liberal Legislation and the Freedom of Contract*. In this he supports the new liberal case for **state** intervention in regulating labour, health and education.

He is best known for his *Lectures on the Principles of Political Obligation*, delivered in 1879 and published after his death in 1882. Here he defends **democracy** in terms of the state, an institution that he sees as based upon will rather than **force**. He rejects **utilitarianism** and argues for a moral life.

See also: **idealism, state, utilitarianism**
Further reading: Richter 1964

Greer, Germaine (1939–) Born in Australia and educated at the universities of Melbourne, Sydney and Cambridge. A rigorous Catholic education helped her to renounce the Church and to embrace sexual liberationism.

Her *Female Eunuch* (1970) created an enormous stir, and in *The Obstacle Race* (1979) she discusses the social and financial difficulties faced by women painters. Her book *Daddy, We Hardly Knew You* (1989) is a family memoir, while her recent *Whole Woman* (1999) (which her contemporary Camille Paglia called 'seriously unbalanced' in the *New York Times*) shows that her views in many respects have not changed.

She is seen by many feminists as an anachronism who relies upon media coverage to keep her brand of 1960s and 1970s **feminism** alive. In her latest work *The Beautiful Boy* (2003) she includes a defence of underage sex tourism guaranteed to raise as many moral hackles as does her contention that female circumcision is no different in principle to an operation for breast cancer.

She is currently Professor of English and Comparative Literature at the University of Warwick and appears frequently in media programmes on both literature and sexuality. A respected academic, she has written about art, literature, abortion and infertility, and the menopause. Her appearances on cultural chat shows have led to feisty confrontations. Angela Carter described her as 'a clever fool'. Margaret Cook called her 'paranoid' and 'a bit obsessive' and Edwina Currie called her 'a great big hardboiled prat'. In 1989 she resigned from teaching at Newnham, Cambridge when a male-to-female transsexual was appointed Fellow at her women-only college.

Further reading: Greer 1999

H

Habermas, Jürgen (1929–) Born in Gummersbach, Germany. In 1964 he was made Professor of Philosophy and Sociology at the University of Frankfurt.

In *Knowledge and Human Interests* (1968), his first major work, Habermas argued that interests inevitably play a role in determining the nature and shape of scientific investigation. He attacked the positivist model of science as ethically neutral and purely technical, and he sought to develop traditions in social philosophy that stretch back to the beginnings of the Enlightenment.

In 1971 he became co-director of the newly created Max Planck Institute for the Study of the Conditions of Life in the Scientific-Technical World. His *Legitimation Crisis*, written in the early 1970s, argued that **capitalism** was experiencing severe problems but declined to identify a social force which would advance an emancipatory solution to these problems. In 1981 he published *The Theory of Communicative Action* in which he maintained that a humane collective life depends on the vulnerable forms of innovation-bearing, reciprocal and egalitarian everyday communication. But Habermas is condemned by his postmodern critics for presenting a 'grand narrative', and he has in turn taken issue with what he sees as the irrationalist, nihilist and neo-conservative tendencies within **postmodernism**.

Habermas's most sustained and substantial treatment of what he regards as the flaws and dangers of postmodernism was presented in his twelve lectures on *The Philosophical Discourse of Modernity* (1985). Habermas's mentor, Adorno, had held that there was a fundamental flaw in the logic of modernity and it gave rise to domination. For Habermas there is no historical necessity for domination in the specific forms of *Zweckrationalität* (instrumental reason) that prevail in the modern world.

See also: **postmodernism**

Further reading: Outhwaite 1994

Hayek, Friedrich (1899–1992) Born in Vienna. He studied law and economics at the University of Vienna.

He became the first director of the Austrian Institute of Economic Research after the First World War, and was appointed to a chair at the London School of Economics in 1931.

In 1944 he published *The Road to Serfdom* that argued that economic planning always led to totalitarian rule. Humans cannot design their own society since each individual is inevitably ignorant of the long-term consequences of particular actions.

The **market** embodies **freedom** and spontaneity.

In 1948 he brought out *Individualism and the Economic Order* in which he built upon von Mises's work to argue that only the market can fruitfully harness knowledge of individuals. He defended a methodology based upon the limited understanding of individuals, and argued that the methods of the natural sciences cannot be applied to understanding human behaviour.

In 1950 he was appointed a Professor of Economics at the University of Chicago (a post that he held until 1962). It was during this period that he published his *Constitution of Liberty*, in which he defended a resolutely negative view of freedom. A free society is of necessity a society dedicated to free enterprise, and Hayek is hostile to the notion of 'social **justice**'. A **democracy** is only desirable if it is based on the market.

He pursued this argument in his three-volume *Law, Legislation and Liberty* (1973–9) where he attacks the 'distorting' effects of interest groups, and advocates a new liberal constitution.

His more recent work deals with questions of money, and what he saw as the fallacies of John Maynard Keynes. He has been hugely influential on the **New Right** and received a knighthood from the Thatcher **government**.

See also: **democracy, New Right**
Further reading: Gray, J. 1984

Hegel, G(eorg) W(ilhelm) F(riedrich) (1770–1831) Born in Stuttgart. The son of a **government** clerk, Hegel studied theology at the University in Tübingen, working as a private tutor in Berne and Frankfurt, before becoming a university lecturer at Jena. He was appointed professor at the University of Heidelberg for two years in 1816, and then acquired the chair of philosophy in Berlin that he held until his death in 1831.

Hegel's theory is steeped in rationalism. He saw the power of reason as unlimited but identified this rational world as consisting ultimately of soul or mind. This world is real in that it exists outside the minds of individuals, but reality itself is ultimately ideal rather than material in character.

This reality passes through a series of **dialectical** categories, and hence the dialectical process – although in theory infinite in its 'unfolding' – is tied to an unhistorical notion of divinity. In *The Philosophy of Right* Hegel was particularly concerned with the **state**. The critical potential of dialectics fizzles out into **conservatism**, since Hegel takes it for granted that private **property**, the **market** and the state are here to stay.

See also: **dialectics, state, property, market**
Further reading: Avineri 1972

hegemony A term that can be used in at least two (conflicting) ways. Either it means domination through superior **power** or **force**, or it means **leadership** usually with an emphasis upon moral and intellectual qualities.

In the first of these uses – domination through force and power – it can be said that in the twenty-first century the USA exercises hegemony throughout the world. China under **Mao** (between 1966 and 1976) frequently charged the then USSR with great power hegemony, that is the use of power to bully and coerce the weak.

The use of the term by **Lenin**, however, implies leadership as in the notion of the workers exercising 'hegemony' over the peasantry. **Gramsci** developed the concept in a distinctive way so that hegemony referred to intellectual and moral leadership, the ideological rather than the coercive aspects of **state** power. Hegemony was given a cultural twist, so that class hegemony referred to the rule of a particular **class** in its ability to capture the 'hearts and minds' of those it controlled. In **Eurocommunism** the term implied either an electoral road to power, or at least political pressure of a kind that respected and worked within liberal norms.

The problem with this usage is that it implies that **coercion** and **consent** can be neatly spliced apart in the analysis of the state. In fact the state is better defined as an institution that uses force to tackle conflicts of interest. If by hegemony we mean moral and intellectual leadership, this hegemony can only really come into its own when the state itself has ceased to exist, and **conflicts** can be resolved through arbitration and negotiation. Policies could then be said to be hegemonic in the Gramscian sense of the term.

See also: **power, force, Lenin, leadership, Gramsci, state, Eurocommunism**

Further reading: Adamson 1980

Heidegger, Martin (1889–1976) Born in Baden, Germany, and studied philosophy at the University of Freiburg. He began teaching in 1915 and worked with Husserl, the founder of phenomenology.

He taught at the University of Marburg between 1923 and 1928, and in 1927 he published his most famous work, *Being and Time*. Influenced by Kierkegaard and **Nietzsche** he argued that the question of Being lies at the heart of philosophy. Western philosophy since **Plato** had culminated in technology and the positive sciences, and this led to a nihilism and wholesale subjectivism. He rejected all accounts of human activity that assume the existence of a human nature. Humans have been thrown into a world they have not made, and they are in continual danger of being swallowed up in a world of mere objects.

In the 1930s he became affiliated to national socialism, and although there is much controversy over his political views at this time, he himself stated that the Nazi movement represented an opportunity for the 'inner recollection and renewal' of the German people. However, his own national socialism differed from the official doctrines of the Nazis, and in his *An Introduction to Metaphysics* that he wrote in 1953, he argued that the 'inner truth and greatness' of national socialism had been obscured by Nazi propagandists. He resigned as Rector of the University of Freiburg in 1934.

After the Second World War he concerned himself more with non-political responses to nihilism. Technology, he complained, has led to a denial of the world and only a poetic and meditative approach can offer solace. We need to return to the deeper understanding of Being offered by the pre-Socratic Greek philosophers.

See also: **Nietzsche**

Further reading: Murray 1978

hermeneutics The term relates to a particular kind of understanding. This concept was originally concerned with biblical interpretation, but it has come to exist as a theoretical approach in **politics** and the social sciences.

The approach is concerned with understanding meaning. It takes the view that humans interpret the world, so that the methods of the natural sciences cannot satisfactorily account for human activity. Hermeneutics seeks to understand meaning in relationship to a wider context. Meaning is part and parcel of a particular society so that texts cannot be understood outside of the culture that informs them. Thus, to understand **Plato,** for example, we need to understand the assumptions he was making in terms of the culture of his time.

We must not assume that texts have a fixed meaning that is somehow independent of the person interpreting them.

But it could be argued that the meaning of a text is a reflection of a world that exists independently of the intentions of the author or reader. People's motives must be taken into account but these motives cannot by themselves account for the significance of what people do. Some seek to make hermeneutics more plausible by arguing that there exist wider cultural meanings of which a particular author may be unaware, but the problem still seems to be that we have to accept uncritically the assumptions of a particular author. It is difficult to see how an objective and critical account of a person's ideas is possible unless one argues that the meaning a person places upon their ideas is simply one piece of evidence among many.

Further reading: Bhaskar 1979

hierarchy A term that denotes **leadership** and differentiation.

Hierarchies are taken for granted in pre-liberal thought, but the term acquires a negative connotation with the development of **liberalism.** Here it is assumed that each individual exists on their own and therefore, in this abstract world, there is absence of hierarchy.

In fact, it could be argued that hierarchies are inherent in **relationships,** since all relationships involve roles in which one person or group leads another. Hierachies are compatible with **freedom, equality** and **democracy,** provided they are fluid and changeable. A patient will defer to a doctor, but should the patient be a motor mechanic and the doctor needs his or her car fixing, then the hierarchy is reversed. It is only when hierarchies are fixed and extend over multiple relationships, that they become oppressive and authoritarian.

Anarchists are wrong therefore to oppose hierarchy *per se*, since it is impossible to conceptualise human relationships without hierarchies.

See also: **liberalism, relationship**

Further reading: Hoffman 2004

historical materialism This refers to the Marxist theory of society.

It is a matter of considerable argument as to whether historical materialism is a theory that applies only to **capitalism**, or can be used to interpret history as a whole.

The theory argues that social life is based upon material production. People have to produce goods and services in order to survive, and an important distinction has to be made between the *forces* and *relations* of production. The forces of production refer to the technology and science involved in the production process such as the use of machinery and computers in contemporary workplaces. The relations of production refer to questions of ownership and control, so that **Marx** believed that under capitalism, for example, there was a growing conflict between socialised forces of production and their ownership by particular individuals.

The theory asserts that in all societies there is a tension between the forces and relations of production, but in **class**-divided societies this tension reaches antagonistic proportions, since particular groups have a vested interest in perpetuating a set of productive relations. The antagonism between the forces and relations of production is, for Marx, the reason why **revolution** is inevitable, although it has to be said that in all societies some tension between the two will exist.

This is why Marx believed that a communist society is

not the end of history (although many scholars interpret his theory in this way), but a new stage in which humanity can consciously control its development.

See also: **revolution**

Further reading: Cohen 1978

Hobbes, Thomas (1588–1679) Born in Wiltshire. He went to Oxford and became tutor to the son of the Earl of Devonshire.

Between 1610 and 1615 he accompanied his pupil to the Continent, visiting Venice. He worked with Bacon and translated the work of the ancient Greek historian Thucydides. In 1630 he joined a group of philosophers in Paris and was greatly influenced by the work of Descartes.

In 1640 he published his *Elements of Law*, and two years later, a Latin text *De Cive*. Here he still defended the position of the Church of England, but he changed his mind in the *Leviathan*, written in 1649–50. By taking the view that a sovereign state was superior to an established church, he upset the Anglican clergy. This position got him into some difficulties after 1660 (when the Church of England had its powers restored), and he also regarded the common lawyers and scientists of the Royal Society as challenging what he saw as the **sovereignty** of the **state**.

Leviathan argues the case that all have a natural right to preserve themselves and should be governed by a **natural** law that seeks peace. Although Hobbes favoured the royalists during the civil war and saw monarchy as the form of the state to be preferred, his radical defence of **individualism** made his theory liberal rather than conservative. He projected a state of nature in which war, not peace, was inevitable, and assumed that people would recognise the need for a sovereign state out of their own self-interest. Human nature was made by a creator but needed to be analysed in completely materialist terms. The state was a 'mortal god' and God himself simply provided support for natural law.

Hobbes has been hugely influential and the idea that without the sovereign state, order is impossible has become a (contestable) part of conventional political theory.

See also: **sovereignty, state**

Further reading: Raphael 1977

humanism A theory that argues that all humans are capable of **freedom**. It develops as the medieval world comes to a close in Europe.

It is linked to **liberalism** historically, and assumes that it is possible to speak of the individual and humankind in universal terms.

The radical potential of humanism is, it could be argued, blunted by its abstract character. Under the influence of liberalism and the Enlightenment, humanity 'shrinks' to **property**-owning males of a particular ethnicity and religion, and it is only gradually that the idea of humankind becomes more inclusive.

A distinction should be made between abstract and concrete humanism. The latter accepts **difference** as an attribute that is positive and seeks to incorporate all human beings. Humanism was caricatured by **Althusser** who developed a theoretical anti-humanism, as though general emancipatory goals conflict with specifically socialist ones. Postmodernists have sometimes seen humanism as inherently abstract, arguing that the theory assumes a static essence and operates a conceptual closure.

In fact humanism is a **momentum concept** since it is impossible to see the attributes of humanity as fixed and frozen. We are continually discovering new aspects that are linked to our humanity, and will continue to do so into the future.

See also: **liberalism, difference, Althusser, momentum concept**
Further reading: Davies 1997

Hume, David (1711–76) Born in Edinburgh. He studied at the University of Edinburgh. In France he composed *A Treatise on Human Nature*, but when the book was published in Britain, it was largely ignored. He sought to present his arguments in a more accessible form, publishing *An Enquiry Concerning Human Understanding* in 1748 and *An Enquiry Concerning the Principles of Morals* in 1751.

He argues that all knowledge derives from sense experience, so that moral judgements rest ultimately upon feelings, useful for social cohesion, but empirically unverifiable. Hume therefore embraced a scepticism that sees uniformity as simply the result of the convergence of beliefs.

Hume had already published his *Essays Moral and Political* in 1742 and ten years later, he produced his *Political Discourses*. Here he attacks the classical liberal notion of the **social contract**, arguing that the **state** arises through circumstance and not as the result of rational agreement. **Justice** develops because people need stability in their possessions.

He was unable to secure an academic post, but between 1754 and 1761 he wrote eight volumes of his *History of England*. He generally favoured free **governments**, by which he meant states that encouraged commerce, the arts and sciences. He supported a stable state from a conservative view based upon scepticism towards dogmas of any kind.

In 1763 he was a secretary in the British embassy in Paris, and Under-Secretary of State in the Northern Department in 1767. His *Dialogues Concerning Natural Religion* was published posthumously in 1779.

See also: **state, justice**
Further reading: Miller 1981

I

idealism A view of the world that sees reality as ultimately composed of ideas rather than as a realm existing outside of consciousness. Idealism argues that because human activity is conscious activity, the real world itself can never be more than a world of ideas.

All religious attitudes, conventionally understood, are idealist in character, but they can be described as forms of *objective idealism*. Objective idealism does not doubt the existence of a reality outside of the individual mind, but sees the real world as the creation of gods or God, so that worshipping God or appeasing the gods is essential for the human control over nature. In its 'deist' form, objective idealism argues that while the world is ultimately created by God, science studies its regularities and character without assuming any further divine intervention.

Objective idealism needs to be distinguished from *subjective idealism*. Subjective idealists argue that the real world is created by individual ideas. Since all data must be processed by the human mind, it is impossible to prove that there is a world beyond these data.

It could be argued that idealism in general is unable to provide an analysis as to how consciousness itself is a product of history.

Further reading: Engels, 1968

ideology Often used as a negative term that denotes authoritarian, dogmatic thought. Ideology is seen as an extremist point of view, and it gets in the way of realistic and moderate thought. However, the term can be taken simply to refer to a belief system whether dogmatic or not.

Marx appears to use the term pejoratively as well although he seems to see ideologies as thoughts that conceal material **interests**. It could be argued, however, that as with the term 'philosophy', Marx was not opposed to the notion of ideology as such. What he objected to were ideologies that turned the world upside down and asserted that pure ideals prevailed rather than particular social interests. Certainly **Lenin** and later Marxists have used the term in a neutral fashion, seeing an ideology as a belief system, and speaking of **Marxism** itself as an ideology.

Some of the negativity in the term can be preserved if we link ideology to the **state**. States, it could be argued, compel people to think in absolutist and ultimate terms (as we would expect from an institution claiming a monopoly of legitimate **force**), so that a post-ideological age would be one in which differences could be settled without the use of force.

See also: **state, force**
Further reading: McLellan 1995

imperialism This term generally denotes political domination or economic exploitation.

As a term designating political domination, it relates to the formation of empires. In this sense the old Soviet Union can be seen as an imperialist power because of its domination over Eastern Europe.

Marxists do not dispute that imperialism can take the form of political domination, but see its basis in **capitalism**, when free competition engenders large-scale corporations described as 'monopolies'. These monopolies seek protection from the **state**, and pressurise the latter into expanding into territories that it then controls. **Lenin's** famous analysis of imperialism drew upon the theories of the liberal thinker, Hobson, and Lenin argued that the monopolies sought external **markets** for their investment having exhausted domestic outlets.

More recently, the term has been used to describe the 'dependency' of the undeveloped third world upon the advanced industrial societies, and imperialism is seen as the manipulation of terms of trade to the disadvantage of the poorer countries. Here imperialism is not tied to the development of 'monopolies' in the late nineteenth century, but is regarded as endemic in the capitalist system from a much earlier period.

With the process of decolonisation since the Second World War, the term has been broadened to account for countries that dominate others through economic controls and political manipulation.

It is significant that after the recent war in Iraq, some commentators have begun to refer to the American empire. Here imperialism is used both pejoratively in terms of the argument that ascribes the war to pressure from the oil industry, as well as positively from those who believe that the United States as an imperial power seeks to extend its norms of '**democracy**' to the Middle Eastern region.

See also: **state, Lenin**
Further reading: Warren 1980

individualism A concept that sees society in terms of individuals. It is a view that only really becomes central with the development of **liberalism**.

Pre-liberal thought, whether ancient or medieval, had no notion of the individual as a universal entity and it is said that the ancients, for example, had no word that expressed this reality.

The problem with liberal individualism, it could be argued, is that it leaves out many individuals. Workers, women and foreigners are often regarded historically as non-individuals, and it is only with the rise of democratic pressure that the concept of the individual has been extended.

The notion of the individual sometimes has the connotation of uniqueness, and this usage is useful provided it does not assume that only some individuals are unique, whereas others are part of an undifferentiated 'mass'.

Individuals do not exist, as classical liberalism assumed, in splendid isolation from one another, but acquire their identity through **relationships**. It is therefore wrong to postulate the individual against the group or collectivity, since individuals cannot exist except as parts of a wider whole.

One individual can only claim individuality if they respect the individuality of others. Exploitation is a negation rather than a product of individualism, since both parties in an exploitative encounter lose their individuality (albeit in different ways). When the individual suffers, the whole group, nation and world is impoverished as a consequence, since the well-being of each is necessarily related to the well-being of all.

See also: **liberalism, relationship**

Further reading: Lukes 1973

interests Interests derive from an individual or group's commitment to a particular conception of their well-being.

The concept is a modern one. Interests may conflict without there being any obvious answer as to which is 'right' or 'wrong', and hence the notion assumes that absolutist standards of **morality** linked to theology have crumbled.

Is there a conflict between what a person prefers and

what is in their interest? It can be argued that the tension between preferences and interests arises in situations in which people are deprived of information as to the consequences of their action. As long as further inputs of information cause a person to alter their preferences, then it can be argued that the tension between interests and preferences is compatible with democratic norms. However, when further inputs of information cease to alter a person's preferences, it has to be conceded that a person is acting in accordance with their interests.

However, it does not follow that an individual interest automatically harmonises with the **common interests** of society. A **conflict** between individual and common interests suggests that the action of an individual, wittingly or unwittingly, harms the interests of large numbers of other individuals. In this case, an action against the offending individual is likely, either in terms of **force** or social pressure. Non-smokers, for example, may insist that even though an individual wishes to harm their own health, it is not acceptable that they should smoke in a way that harms the health of others.

Conflicts of interest are inevitable in a society, and the notion of 'common interests' should not be taken to imply an absence of conflict, but refers rather to the kind of conflict that allows for disputes to be settled without the use of force.

See also: **conflict**
Further reading: Flathman 1966

J

Jacobinism The term derives from the group which set up a club during the French **Revolution** of 1789. The revolutionary Jacobins met in the old convent in the Rue

St Jacques (and the Latin for Jacques or James is Jacobus). The Jacobins were committed to principles of what they considered 'extreme **democracy** and absolute **equality**'. Under the leadership of Robespierre they imposed the Reign of Terror between 1793 and 1794, when opponents, real or suspected, were ruthlessly denounced and executed.

In the nineteenth century the term was used by conservatives to designate anyone who was concerned with radical political reform. But **Marx** was critical of the Jacobins for seeking to destroy private **property** through the will of the **state**, without understanding its links with **capitalism**. The term Jacobin, on the left, came to mean a revolutionary who jumped the stages of history, and believed that revolutions could be made through the dedicated efforts of an elite.

Lenin is frequently called a Jacobin, and it is true that he speaks admiringly of the Jacobins, and their willingness to use violence. However, strictly speaking, Lenin followed the Marxist theory that revolution requires material conditions to mature, although the Bolshevik revolution of 1917 was seen by its critics as a Jacobin seizure of **power**, that is, a revolution made in conditions that had not matured. Evidence of this Jacobinism was also found in the dictatorial manner in which the Bolsheviks sustained their rule.

Gramsci used 'Jacobin' to denote a Marxist who subscribed to the theory of permanent revolution – the belief that a bourgeois revolution can rapidly develop into a proletarian one – and he took the view that such theory was irrelevant for Western Europe where capitalism ruled through powerful cultural apparatuses, like the media, the party and educational system.

See also: **Lenin, Gramsci, property, state, capitalism**
Further reading: Harding 1996

Jefferson, Thomas (1743–1826) Born in Virginia. He studied at the William and Mary College in Williamsburg.

He was elected to Virginian legislature in 1769 and in his *A Summary View of the Rights of British America* he drew upon **Locke's** theory of natural right to argue that the British Crown must act as an impartial arbiter over the legislatures in the Empire. He was a delegate to the Continental Congress, and in 1776 drafted the Declaration of Independence.

He was Governor of Virginia from 1779 to 1781, and in 1785 he became Minister of Finance. With Washington as the first President, Jefferson became Secretary of State. His *Notes on Virginia* was published in 1785. He found himself increasingly at odds with Hamilton's centralist policies, and in 1797 he was elected Vice President when Adams became President.

Jefferson took the view that democratic communities needed to be small and encouraged the division of Virginia into areas of 5 to 6 square miles with 100 citizens in each. Land should be given to citizens so that local direct **democracy** resembling an ancient Greek *polis* could be established. Although a slave owner himself, Jefferson was opposed to **slavery**.

Deeply religious, he advocated freedom of religion. He did not accept the participation of women in **politics**.

In 1800 he was elected President and in 1803 he persuaded Congress to support exploration to the west of the Mississippi, and in his second term of office prohibited any further importation of slaves. In his retirement he helped to establish the University of Virginia.

See also: **Locke, democracy, slavery, politics**
Further reading: Cunningham 1987

justice Justice is not simply goodness or virtue: it involves giving every person their due.

Thus if a person is 'justly' punished, then they have to be found guilty of wrongdoing through transparent and acceptable procedures; these penalties should be uniform, and the punishment must be deemed 'to fit the crime'. The problem with this punitive notion of justice is that it is hard therefore to see how such punishments will resolve conflicts of interest.

Justice, it could be argued, implies development, so that the question of how the individual should be given his or her due depends upon how they may best be developed in a particular context.

Pre-modern notions of justice saw the **market** itself as problematic and argued the case for a 'just price' – an exchange that took account of social position of those party to the exchange. The notion returns in the concept of 'social justice' – a concern that the distribution of resources must be fair. Here supporters of 'social justice' divide as to whether the criterion for distribution is based upon merit and desert, or upon need. Need must be defined in a way that takes account of biological and developmental needs. As for merit and desert, they are valuable criteria if taken seriously. Can it be said that a person who inherits wealth 'deserves' it, even though it is merely their good luck that they were born into a particular family?

Those who see the market as central as a mechanism of distribution reject the whole notion of 'social justice'. But it could well be argued that increasingly inequality is destructive of social **relationships**, so that the just society must pay attention to the deliberate distribution of resources.

See also: **market, relationship**

Further reading: Campbell 1988

K

Kant, Immanuel (1724–1804) Born in Königsberg in East Prussia, where at 16 he entered the University.

He published his first work in 1749 and then worked as a tutor. When he returned to the university in 1755, he published *Universal Natural History and Theory of the Heavens*, a much more successful scientific work than his first. The following year Kant published a work on natural philosophy that made him eligible for a salaried professorship, although he was not to receive one until 1770. In these years, Kant also published four essays on earthquakes and winds.

Kant began lecturing in the autumn of 1755, but except for one small essay on optimism (1759), he did not publish again until 1762, when a further four publications earned Kant widespread recognition in Germany.

Kant was appointed Professor of Logic and Metaphysics in Königsberg in 1770. Beginning in 1781, with the first edition of the *Critique of Pure Reason*, he unleashed a steady torrent of books. He sought to present 'reason' as a force that was autonomous from the world of experience.

From a **politics** point of view, the most significant of these include his two essays 'Idea for a Universal History from a Cosmopolitan Point of View' and 'What is Enlightenment?' In 1784 he also published *The Groundwork of the Metaphysics of Morals*. In 1793 he wrote the political essay 'On the Common Saying: "That may be right in theory but does not work in practice"', and *Towards Perpetual Peace* appeared in 1795, a work that defended cosmopolitanism in a world of republican states. By cosmopolitanism, Kant meant an outlook that focussed on the **interests** of people everywhere.

Further reading: Cassirer 1982

Kautsky, Karl (1854–1938) Born in Prague and educated at the University of Vienna.

After living in Zurich and London, Kautsky founded the socialist paper *Neue Zeit*, in 1883. He joined the Social Democratic Party and drafted the Erfurt Programme.

In 1887 he published *The Economic Doctrines of Karl Marx* and a year later, *Thomas Moore and His Utopia*. In 1895 he published *The Forerunners of Modern Socialism* where he reviewed socialist ideas from **Plato** to the French **Revolution**. In the *Agrarian Question* in 1899 he argued that the peasantry was becoming increasingly proletarianised as a result of capitalist development. **Capitalism**, he argued, was continually exhausting its **markets** and hence bound to collapse.

In 1906 his *Ethics and the Materialist Conception of History* exhibited his strong adherence to Darwinism as he focussed on the biological and social basis for moral ideas. He was considered the 'Pope of Marxism', and was fiercely critical of **Bernstein**'s 'revisionist' arguments. He saw himself as a theorist of the 'centre' and balanced his critique of Bernstein with a critical analysis of the ideas of **Luxemburg**, arguing that the notion of mass strikes did not square with the commitment to parliamentary institutions and **democracy**.

He opposed Germany's participation in the First World War, but was sharply critical of the Russian Revolution, and became the target of **Lenin**'s wrath. Kautsky continued to see himself as an orthodox Marxist and saw Leninism as a deviation from the classical tradition.

His work on *The Materialist Interpretation of History* published in 1927 was written at a time in which social democrats had decisively broken from communists, and there was little interest from this section of the left in the Marxist tradition.

See also: **Plato, Bernstein, Luxemburg, Lenin**

Further reading: Geary 1987

Kropotkin, Peter (1842–1921) Born into an aristocratic family. His father was an officer in the imperial army, and Kropotkin attended the most select military academy in Russia. He then became a military administrator in Eastern Siberia, concluding, in his observation of the natural world, that cooperation is the most important factor in evolution.

It was in Siberia that Kropotkin became an anarchist. He returned to St Petersburg in 1867 and enthusiastically welcomed the Paris Commune in 1871. His anti-authoritarianism was confirmed by what he saw as **Marx**'s autocratic handling of the dispute with **Bakunin** in the First International. For two years he worked closely with a populist group called the Chaikovsky circle, publishing a manifesto in 1873 entitled *Must We Occupy Ourselves with the Ideal of a Future System?* He was imprisoned for three years but he escaped and wrote a number of pamphlets and helped set up the journal *Le Révolté*.

In 1882 he was sentenced to five years' imprisonment by the French authorities, but was released in 1886 following an international outcry. The following year he wrote *In Russian and French Prisons*, having settled in London. He was active in anarchist **politics** and had a high reputation as a scientist. He opposed indiscriminate violence but was not a pacifist. In 1892 he published *The Conquest of Bread* in Paris, and seven years later published his *Memoirs of a Revolutionist*.

He supported Britain and France during the First World War. He returned to Russia after the **Revolution**, and although he was opposed to the 'dictatorial tendencies' of the Bolsheviks, argued against foreign intervention. When he died, he was offered a state funeral, but his family refused.

See also: **Marx, Bakunin**
Further reading: Miller 1976

L

leadership Leadership can only arise when there are followers. Hence it is a necessary part of a **relationship**. The existence of leadership can only be denied by those who reject the need for individuals to develop through **relationships** with one another.

The notion of leadership is taken for granted by preliberal thought since **hierarchy** is seen as **natural** and people are differentiated according to the roles they play. Rulers lead the ruled; men lead women; lords lead their serfs; citizens lead slaves and so on. Leadership is preordained.

These notions are challenged by **liberalism**. In the place of hierarchical relationships, there is abstract **equality**. The relationship is not one of **difference**, but of sameness. Strictly speaking, classical liberalism is opposed to the concept of leadership because, as a theory, it places individuals outside of relationships. Abstract **individualism**, it could be argued, makes the notion of leadership theoretically impossible, and it is this abstract individualism that leads anarchists to argue that individuals can spontaneously govern themselves without organisation or hierarchy.

Post-liberal or relational argument accepts leadership as inevitable, since what makes a relationship possible is that *on a particular issue* one person leads and the other follows. For this reason, relationships are necessarily hierarchical – two people can only relate to one another because they are both the same and different – and this difference must generate deference of some kind. But although post-liberalism stresses the relational character of human activity, it differs from pre-liberal thought in that the notion of leadership as **natural** is tied to a concept of nature that is developmental and not static.

Leaders and followers continually change places. Leadership is always provisional and specific – a leader who is developmental in one area becomes oppressive when he or she seeks to guide in every issue. Leaders in a **democracy** dedicate themselves to enhancing the capacity of people to govern their own lives.

See also: **relationship, hierarchy, natural, liberalism, equality, difference, individualism, democracy**

Further reading: Adair 1973

legitimacy Legitimacy refers to the acceptance of rules and procedures that limit the action of those making and implementing these rules and procedures.

Legitimacy may derive from tradition or from the charisma of **leaderships**. In its modern form, it derives from procedures that are transparent and regular.

Only with **liberalism** does the notion of acceptance receive refinement, so that legitimacy becomes a law or rule to which subjects have consented. However, the liberal tradition, it could be argued, treats this question in an elitist manner, so that legitimacy historically is an attribute that concerns male **property** owners and is merely ascribed to everyone else.

What is legitimate is *limited*. Rules that are not accepted are not limited and are not legitimate. Legitimacy thus requires compliance, and compliance that has not resulted from duress. Where **force** is credibly threatened or used, then legitimacy cannot arise.

Legitimate force is thus a contradiction in terms. Force cannot be realistically limited, however much liberal **states** and societies might try. If we define the state as an institution using force to tackle conflicts of interest, then the legitimacy of the state itself is impossible. We could certainly agree that the attempt to render force legitimate is preferable to a situation in which no attempt is made at all, but force itself (and the credible threat of this force) cannot be squared with the concept of legitimacy.

It is argued that legitimacy for some might mean illegitimacy for others, but if legitimacy is a **relationship**, then a lack of legitimacy contaminates both parties (albeit in different ways), so that an act that is illegitimate to a subordinate cannot be meaningfully carried through, and hence is not legitimate for the ruler either.

See also: **liberalism, force, state, relationship**
Further reading: Beetham 1991

Lenin, Vladimir Ilyich (1870–1924) Born Ulyanov in Simbirsk, Russia, he was educated at the local gymnasium. Expelled from Kazan University, he studied law in St Petersburg.

In 1895 he formed the Union of Struggle for the Emancipation of the Working Class. In 1896 Lenin was arrested and sentenced to three years' internal exile, where he wrote *The Development of Capitalism in Russia*, *The Tasks of Russian Social Democrats*, as well as articles for various socialist journals.

Released in 1900, Lenin moved to Geneva and became involved with *Iskra*, the official paper of the Social Democratic Labour Party. In 1902 Lenin published *What is to be Done?* in which he argued for a party of professional revolutionaries dedicated to the overthrow of

Tsarism. His long-time friend Martov disagreed, and won the vote 28–23 but Lenin was unwilling to accept the result and formed a faction known as the Bolsheviks. Those who remained loyal to Martov became known as Mensheviks.

After the failure of the 1905 **Revolution,** Lenin called on Bolsheviks to participate in the elections for the Russian Parliament or Duma (a legislature with limited powers). In 1913 he moved to Galicia in Austria, but was arrested the following year as a Russian spy. After a brief imprisonment he was allowed to move to Switzerland, where he branded the First World War as an **imperialist** conflict and wrote *Imperialism: The Highest Stage of Capitalism.*

In March 1917, the Tsar abdicated. Lenin travelled to Petrograd (today St Petersburg) and in his *April Theses* he argued for a socialist revolution. Kerensky, head of the Provisional Government, gave orders for Lenin's arrest. Lenin escaped to Finland where he completed his *State and Revolution*, a pamphlet that made the case for soviet (or council) rule in Russia. Lenin returned to Petrograd, and when Kerensky moved to crush the Bolsheviks, the Winter Palace was stormed and the Cabinet ministers arrested.

In October 1917, Lenin was elected chairman of the Soviet Council of People's Commissars. Land was distributed to peasants. Banks were nationalised and workers' control of factory production introduced. The Assembly elected to draw up a new constitution, was closed down, other political parties were banned, and in 1918 with German troops moving towards Petrograd, Lenin ordered **Trotsky** to sign the Brest-Litovsk Treaty which resulted in the surrender of the Ukraine, Finland, the Baltic provinces, the Caucasus and Poland. Civil war followed, and in 1919 there was an uprising against the Bolsheviks at Kronstadt. Lenin now introduced the New

Economic Policy that allowed some **market** trading and denationalisation.

After being shot by a member of the Socialist Revolutionaries, Lenin's health declined and in April 1922, **Stalin** occupied the new post of General Secretary. An operation left Lenin paralysed, three days after dictating a 'will and testament', in which he called for the removal of Stalin from the post of General Secretary.

See also: **imperialism, Trotsky, market, Stalin**
Further reading: Harding 1981

liberalism A theory that postulates the (abstract) **freedom** and **equality** of all individuals. Essentially a modern outlook, liberalism in its classical form presented individuals as living outside both **state** and society.

However, even when liberals came to accept that individuals have always lived in a society, they continue to operate with a notion of the individual that abstracts him or her (it is usually a him) from social **relationships**. It is this mystification that accounts for the tension between the freedom and equality preached in theory, and historical support for **slavery, patriarchy,** colonialism and the political **power** of the middle classes. Liberals see the **market** as **natural** and the desire to appropriate private **property** is linked to human nature.

Because the notion of private property is necessarily exclusive, liberals accept the need for the state to defend property against those who would 'interfere' with it. However, it could be argued that the reconciliation of freedom and the state is an insoluble problem for liberals, since freedom is (rightly) deemed the absence of **force,** and yet the state, though artificial in most liberal accounts, is seen as necessary.

Liberalism has unwittingly generated a whole range of ideologies that seek to bring liberal theory into accord with social practice. Modern liberals have extended the notion of freedom into social spheres so that in Britain, for example, the architect of the welfare state, Beveridge, was a liberal. Nor do modern liberals see the market as an autonomous, self-regulating entity, but make the case – Keynes was another great British liberal – for intervention by the state. Collective institutions like trade unions and cooperatives play a role in securing social **justice**. In the USA the word 'liberal' is used generally as a synonym for 'modern liberals', and old-fashioned liberals are called 'conservatives'.

Although modern liberals can seem quite close to socialists, they remain concerned to humanise rather transform private property, the market and the state.

See also: **freedom, equality, relationship, slavery, patriarchy, natural, property, state, force**

Further reading: Ramsey 1997

Locke, John (1632–1704) Born near Bristol. He studied medicine and 'natural philosophy' at Oxford.

He joined the household of the Earl of Shaftesbury in 1667 but moved to Holland when the earl was accused of treason during the reign of James II.

When William of Orange became King, Locke returned to England, and published his *Two Treatises of Government*. The *First Treatise* sets out to challenge Sir Robert Filmer's absolutist argument that kings rule through divine right, but the *Second Treatise* has been much more influential. In it Locke argues that all are free and equal by nature, and that rule must derive from their **consent**. He distinguishes between the 'political' **authority** of ruler and ruled and the domination of parent over their children, a man over his wife, and masters over their servants and slaves.

Until a political society is established, humans are governed simply by a law of nature. People captured in war can have their lives spared in return for becoming slaves. Locke assumes that no person may own that which spoils, but with the invention of money, it becomes possible to store value.

When Locke speaks of acquiring **property,** he talks of the need for the owner or the owner's servant to mix labour in with an object. It is clear that growing inequality engenders 'inconveniences'. People come together to form a 'political society'. Locke makes a distinction between 'explicit' as opposed to 'tacit' **consent.** The former would be given by property owners who are citizens and vote in elections, whereas the latter would be the kind of consent that all adults are deemed to express by simply being present in a particular society. Locke is concerned about property owners and argues that when confronted with arbitrary and despotic rule, they have a right of resistance. This right was invoked about a hundred years later by American colonists to justify their rebellion against the British Crown.

In 1690 Locke argues in his *Essay Concerning Human Understanding* that all knowledge derives from the senses and cannot be regarded as innate, and in 1693 Locke shared his *Thoughts on Education* and two years later wrote *On the Reasonableness of Christianity.*

See also: **property, consent**
Further reading: Gough 1973

Lukács, Georg (1885–1971) Born in Budapest. He studied at Berlin and Heidelberg.

He joined the Hungarian Communist Party in the wake of the Russian **Revolution,** and was Commissar of Culture Education during the Hungarian Soviet of 1919. Following its suppression, he fled to Vienna and in 1923 he published *History and Class Consciousness.*

In this book, he attacks 'orthodox **Marxism**' for its theory of reflection, dialectics of nature and its notion of a law-governed history. He criticises the influence of **Engels**, and stresses the importance of self-conscious human activity. He argued that many Marxists had succumbed to a positivist view of science and had embraced a reified and alienated view of the world. The proletariat alone can grasp the 'totality' of society.

Condemned by the Comintern, Lukács retracted many of his propositions. He was in Berlin from 1929 to 1933, before going to Moscow, and becoming a member of the Institute of Philosophy.

He returned to Hungary in 1945 and became a member of parliament and a professor at the University of Budapest. His work on *The Historical Novel* appeared in 1955. In 1956 he served as Minister of Culture in the **government** established by the Hungarian Revolution, and following his arrest and deportation, he was able to return to Budapest in 1957.

As a literary critic, he was fiercely opposed to 'modernism' and defended **realism**, praising Balzac and Scott, for example, as critical writers who alluded to the **conflicts** of their time.

He crossed swords with **Sartre**, condemned structuralism and psychoanalysis and in his *Destruction of Reason* (which appeared in English in 1980) he attacked **Heidegger** for his pro-Nazi sympathies.

See also: **Sartre, Heidegger**

Further reading: Löwy 1979

Luxemburg, Rosa (1871–1919) Born in Zamosc, in the Polish area of Russia. In 1889 she emigrated to Zurich where she studied law and political economy.

While in Switzerland she met other socialist revolutionaries from Russia, and in 1893 helped to form the

Social Democratic Party of Poland. She went to Paris to edit the party's newspaper, *Sprawa Robotnicza* (*Workers' Cause*). She criticised the 'revisionism' of **Bernstein** in her first major work, *Social Reform or Revolution* (1899).

She settled in Berlin where she joined the Social Democratic Party, and in 1905 she became editor of SPD newspaper *Vorwarts* (*Forward*). During the 1905 **Revolution** she returned to Warsaw and the following year published *The Mass Strike, the Political Party, and the Trade Unions*. She argued that a general strike had the power to radicalise the workers and bring about a socialist revolution.

Her book on **imperialism**, *The Accumulation of Capital*, was published in 1913. Although she continued to advocate the need for a violent overthrow of **capitalism**, she took the side of the Mensheviks in their struggle with the Bolsheviks. She opposed Germany's participation in the First World War, and was involved in establishing an underground political organisation called Spartakusbund (Spartacus League). In 1916 she wrote the highly influential pamphlet *The Crisis in the German Social Democracy*, and in the same year she was arrested and imprisoned, following a demonstration in Berlin. It was here that she criticised the dictatorial methods of the Bolsheviks.

She was released in 1918 and was a founding member of the German Communist Party. In 1919, Luxemburg helped organise the Spartakist Rising in Berlin. The army was called in; the rebellion was crushed, and Luxemburg (along with Liebkneckt) was executed without trial.

See also: **capitalism**

Further reading: Geras 1976

Lyotard, Jean-François (1924–88) Born in Vincennes, France, he studied philosophy and literature at the

Sorbonne. His early interest in philosophies of indifference resulted in his MA dissertation *Indifference as an Ethical Notion*. Until the Second World War Lyotard's way of life was, in his own words, 'poetic, introspective and solitary'.

The war disrupted both his way of life and his thought; he acted as a first-aid volunteer in the fight for liberation in the Paris streets in August 1944, and gave up the idea of indifference for a commitment to the investigation of reality in terms of social interactions.

Lyotard passed the *agrégation* (the examination required in order to teach in France) and in 1950 he took up a position teaching philosophy at a boy's lycée (school) in Constantine in French-occupied East Algeria in 1950. From 1952 to 1959 he taught at a school for the sons of military personnel at La Flèche. In Constantine Lyotard read **Marx** and became acquainted with the Algerian political situation, which he believed was ripe for socialist **revolution**.

He wrote a book on phenomenology in 1954. He joined the left-wing *Socialism or Barbarism* group and was their principal spokesperson on Algeria. He broke with them in 1963.

But he became disillusioned both with the reformism of socialism, the authoritarianism of communism and the futility of the far left. In 1974 he published *The Libidinal Economy* but the work for which he is best known, *The Post-Modern Condition: A Report on Knowledge*, was published in 1979. Here he attacks what he calls 'grand narratives' – attempts to present a view of history that seeks to explain the world as a whole. All universals, whether expressed through **nationalism, liberalism, Marxism,** are merely ideological discourses and they deserve our 'incredulity'. The term **'postmodernism'** stems from this work. He spurned the invitation by the Mitterand **government** to debate socialism on the grounds that its 'modernisation' represents precisely the kind of grand narrative that should be rejected.

The Differend: Phrases in Dispute, published in 1983, stressed the heterogeneity of language and perspectives. In *Heidegger and the Jews* that appeared in 1988, he saw in Auschwitz a memorial to an event that must never be forgotten.

He wrote twenty-seven books in all, even contemplating publishing a book with no title or acknowledged author, but desisted because he feared that it would become a valued possession. He taught philosophy at the University of Paris, and French and Italian at the University of California, Irvine. Many of his books have been translated into English and a *Lyotard Reader* appeared in 1989.

See also: **nationalism, liberalism, Marxism, postmodernism**

Further reading: Browning 2000

M

Machiavelli, Niccolò (1469–1527) Born in Florence. During his youth he had watched the reformer Savranola at work and received his first paid employment in the chancery. In 1502 he became secretary to a number of war commissions and a diplomat throughout Europe. He was particularly influenced by Borgia. Borgia was cruel and cunning but Machiavelli felt that he could unite Italy – a goal dear to Machiavelli.

The Prince was dedicated to Lorenzo de' Medici in 1515–16. However, when Medici was restored to office, Machiavelli was briefly imprisoned. The book was committed to a pragmatic view of statecraft, and rejected the idea that the ruler must aspire to Christian **morality**. Where necessity requires, the prince must be prepared to lie. The prince himself must be half-beast and half-man (like the ancient centaur), combining the cunning of the fox with the strength of the lion. *Virtu* in *The Prince* differed from traditional moral virtues, and the effectiveness of the prince depends upon his ability to adapt to *Fortuna* – the changing currents of fortune.

Between 1513 and 1516 Machiavelli composed *The Discourses* – a book that argued the case for a republic as a form of the **state** better adapted to changing circumstances (than monarchies) and providing more opportunity for political and military participation. He based his analysis upon the model of the Roman republic, and he took the view that the masses must ultimately be placated.

In 1521 the *Art of War* appeared and there followed various writings, including a history of Florence. His work was proscribed by the Papacy from 1557 until 1850 and yet the use of the term 'Machiavellian' as a synonym for deceit and corruptions is unjust, when account is taken of the originality of Machiavelli, his **realism** and his commitment to **republicanism**.

See also: **morality, state, republicanism**
Further reading: Skinner 1981

MacKinnon, Catharine (1946–) Born in Minneapolis, Minnesota. She studied law and political science at Smith College and Yale.

In 1979 she published *Sexual Harassment of Working Women: a Case of Sexual Discrimination*. Seven years later she successfully persuaded the US Supreme Court that sexual harassment constituted sexual discrimination for which employers could be sued.

With the feminist activist and writer **Dworkin**, she wrote an anti-pornography ordinance that would have allowed individuals to sue those who sold, produced or distributed material that was deemed harmful. This was approved by the Minnesota city council but vetoed by the mayor. The Supreme Court held that a similar ordinance passed in Indianapolis, Indiana, violated the First Amendment of the Constitution. Many feminists in Britain and the USA took the view that anti-pornography campaigns simply played into the hands of conservatives and were contrary to feminist commitments to **freedom**.

In 1987 she published *Feminism Unmodified* in which she criticised liberal and socialist feminists for linking **feminism** to established ideological positions, and in *Toward a Feminist Theory of the State* she attacks the liberal **state** as inherently patriarchal. Legal norms such as 'fairness' and '**equality**' inevitably privilege men, and **consent** to sexuality is, as far as women are concerned, formal and assumed. She regarded rape as the same as 'normal' sexual activity, and sought to abolish the **public/private divide**. Her work is a classic radical feminist tract that condemns not only **liberalism** but **Marxism** as well, which she sees as a doctrine that naturalises sexual subordination and emancipates only men.

She worked with Croatian and Muslim women in the 1990s, demanding reparations from the Serbian authorities for atrocities against women. In 1994 she published *Only Words*, and in 2006 she wrote *Are Women Human?* in which she focuses particularly on the damage done to women by rape.

See also: **Dworkin, freedom, feminism, equality, liberalism, public/private divide, Marxism**

Further reading: MacKinnon 1989

MacIntyre, Alasdair (1929–) Born in Scotland, and studied in Manchester and London. Having held chairs in sociology at several British universities, he emigrated to the

USA. He has taught at numerous North American universities, and is currently Professor of Philosophy at Duke University.

In 1958 he wrote a work on the unconscious, and in 1966 *A Short History of Ethics*. With Paul Ricoeur he published *The Religious Significance of Atheism* in 1969. A one time Marxist, he published a book on **Marcuse** in 1970.

His work *After Virtue* was published in 1981, and he became known as the theorist of **communitarianism**, but with a position that is anti-liberal and neoclassical in character. He saw **liberalism** as flawed by a moral relativism that is unable to defend a particular point of view, and a specific concept of the Good. This makes it impossible to develop a notion of **morality** and the development of roles and responsibilities. MacIntyre stressed the importance of tradition as encapsulating a particular ethical code.

In *Whose Justice? Whose Rationality?* published in 1988, he argued the case for a value system derived from **Aristotle** and linked to the Christian tradition of Augustine and Aquinas. It could be argued that MacIntyre fails to practise what he preaches since the neoclassicism he expounds, does not embody the **community** traditions of the USA. Moreover it might also be asserted that it is crucial to go beyond rather than simply reject the liberal tradition, and feminists object that his notion of good applies to men rather than women.

In 1990 he wrote *Three Rival Versions of Moral Inquiry*, and in 1999 he published *Dependent Rational Animals: Why Human Beings Need the Virtues*.

He is a corresponding fellow of the British Academy.

See also: **Marcuse, communitarianism, morality, Aristotle**

Further reading: MacIntyre 1981

Macpherson, C(rawford) B(rough) (1911–87) Born in Toronto and educated at the university in this city. He took a Masters at the London School of Economics, and became a lecturer at the University of Toronto in 1936.

He worked for the Canadian Information Board during the war, spending the rest of his academic career in Toronto. He visited Oxford for a couple of sabbaticals and lectured in Israel, Australia, Holland and the United States.

In 1962 he published *The Political Theory of Possessive Individualism*, the work that won him an international reputation. In it he subjected the work of **Hobbes**, **Locke** and other classical liberals to a readable, Marxist critique, and the book was translated into many languages. He had already served on the executive on the International Political Science Association (1950–8), and in 1963 he became President of the Canadian Political Science Association. In 1965 he lectured for the Canadian Broadcasting Corporation and a year later, his lectures appeared as *The Real World of Democracy*. In 1967 he was involved in promoting university reform.

He campaigned against the Vietnam War, having participated in the Canadian peace movement. In 1973 he published his essays on *Democratic Theory* in which he subjected Isaiah **Berlin**'s 'two concepts of liberty' to a fierce critique.

In 1977 he published *The Life and Times of Liberal Democracy*, arguing that liberal **democracy** can go beyond **capitalism**. His models of liberal democracy covered **utilitarianism**, the position of **J. S. Mill**, the theory of elitist democracy put forward by **Schumpeter** and **Dahl**, and expressed a preference for a participatory model.

Macpherson received a number of honorary degrees, and was made an Officer of the Order of Canada in 1976.

See also: **Mill, utilitarianism, Schumpeter, Dahl**
Further reading: Townshend 2000

Madison, James (1751–1836) Born in Virginia. Madison attended the College of New Jersey (now Princeton).

He helped to frame the Virginia Constitution in 1776 and at 36, he was a key participant in the Constitutional Convention at Philadelpia. With Jay and Hamilton, he wrote *The Federalist Papers*, making the case for the ratification of the Constitution. He closely studied ancient as well as modern confederacies, and based his position on a Lockean theory of natural **rights**. He defended majority rule, arguing in the celebrated essay 'No. 10' that representative **government** can overcome the dangers of majoritarian tyranny if there is a variety of parties and **interests** in the electorate. The separation of **government** into three distinct branches can help to overcome any headstrong passion of the legislative body.

He was elected to the new House of Representatives where he served from 1788 to 1797. Here he helped to frame the Bill of Rights. He opposed Hamilton's financial policies that he considered would favour the north, and he played a part in forming the Republican Party that had **Jefferson** elected as President in 1800. He served as Jefferson's Secretary of State until 1809 before becoming President himself.

It was as Secretary of State that he protested vigorously against the French and British seizure of American ships. As President he sought to restrict trade with Britain and in 1812 he declared war. Although the British entered Washington, General Andrew Jackson won a significant victory at New Orleans.

Madison's presidency ended in 1817 and during his retirement, he vigorously opposed those who argued (like

Calhoun) that the rights of individual states should prevail over the acts of the Federal Government.

See also: **government, Jefferson**

Further reading: Epstein 1984

Mao Zedong (1893–1976) Born in Shaoshan, China. His education was part classical and part modern.

He was a soldier during the 1911 **Revolution**, and in Beijing he took a post in a university library. He helped to found the Chinese Communist Party. He had a minor role in the coalition **government** with the Guomindang but became leader of the party after Chiang Kai Shek had purged the Communists.

Mao became increasingly persuaded by the revolutionary potential of the peasantry, and after a number of unsuccessful peasant uprisings, saw any attempt to set up soviets in urban areas as doomed to failure. During the Long March the party moved to the north west, and during the 'rectification' campaign in 1942–3, **leadership** rivals were compelled to criticise their past conduct.

He developed a guerrilla strategy against the invading Japanese (whom the Guomindang saw as less dangerous than the Communists). In 1949 Mao became head of the new People's Republic.

As leader Mao tried but abandoned Soviet methods, and employed social and economic experiments that conflicted with previous Marxist models. Communes were established in 1955, and in 1958–9 the Great Leap Forward sought to mobilise the peasants through moral rather than material incentives. Massive famines resulted as agricultural workers tried to make steel in backyard furnaces. Mao's standing in the party suffered, and to regain lost ground, he launched the Cultural Revolution in 1966 that targeted the intelligentsia and party leadership. The army was forced to intervene in order to restore order, and from then until his death, Chinese **politics** was controlled by rehabilitated party and **state** leaders, members of the armed forces and radicals from the Cultural Revolution.

Further reading: Schram 1983

Marcuse, Herbert (1898–1979) Born in Berlin. He received his doctorate from the University of Freiburg.

In his article 'On the Problem of the Dialectic' (1930) he argued that **Marxism** ignored the practical activity of the individual, and concerned at **Heidegger's** support for the Nazis (he had been greatly influenced by Heidegger), he joined the Frankfurt Institute for Social Research. In 1933 he published the first major review of **Marx's** *Economic and Philosophical Manuscripts*, having worked intensively on **Hegel**. In 1934, when the Nazis seized **power**, he fled to the United States where he lived for the rest of his life.

Reason and Revolution was published in 1941which saw critical theory as a substitute for the proletariat as agent of social transformation. After working for the US **government**, he published *Eros and Civilization* in 1955. Here he sought to draw upon **Freud** to sketch the outlines of a non-repressive society: a vision of liberation that anticipated many of the values of the 1960s.

In 1958, he published a highly critical work on the Soviet Union, *Soviet Marxism*. He made both capitalist and communist societies the target of his famous critique in *One-Dimensional Man* (1964). Here he argued that technological rationality had integrated all individuals into an advanced industrial society that eliminated opposition and escape.

This was followed by his influential piece on *Repressive Tolerance* in 1965. *An Essay on Liberation* followed four years later, and *Counterrevolution and Revolt* was published in 1972. In 1965, Marcuse took a position at the University of California at La Jolla where he remained until his retirement in the 1970s. In his final book, *The Aesthetic Dimension* that appeared in 1979, he saw in art the vision of an emancipatory society.

See also: **Heidegger, Marx, Hegel**

Further reading: Geohegan 1981

market A concept that is more than economic. Markets can exist in every sphere of society where there is scarcity. It could be argued that wherever they exist, they conceal differences in **power** and status.

Obviously markets relate to the exchange of goods and services, but it has become very fashionable under the influence of the New Right to introduce markets into education and health care in liberal societies.

Markets spring up in response to a perceived scarcity, and attempts to suppress the market cannot succeed where goods and service cannot be provided by other institutions in society. The East European experience under communist party rule has confirmed that where need cannot be met in other ways, people will form a market, however informally or illegally.

The presence of the market becomes central in liberal societies and was seen by classical liberals as an autonomous mechanism that is separate from the **state**, and even from society. This view is now discredited.

The problem with the market, it could be argued, is that it masks real differences, so that individuals or groups engaged in exchanges are abstractly equated.

The idea that the market is rooted in human nature is ahistorical and implausible, but it is true that markets have been around for thousands of years. It is argued by theorists on the 'left' that they need to be regulated according to human needs and developments, and their positive side – the emphasis upon agency and initiative – should be emphasised as attempts are made to curb the inequalities that markets generate.

The transformation of the market is a lengthy process, since markets both precede **capitalism** and would continue in a post-capitalist society. However, this transformation arises as markets fail to meet human needs, and society has to find other ways of tackling its problems.

See also: **New Right, state, capitalism**

Further reading: O'Neill 1998

Marshall, T(homas) H(umphrey) (1893–1981) Marshall taught at the London School of Economics (LSE) from 1925 until his retirement in 1956.

He moved to the sociology department in 1929, receiving a readership the following year. He served in the Foreign Office during the war. In 1944 he was appointed Professor of Social Institutions and headed the social science department. He helped to lay the foundations for social class and population studies at the LSE after the war, playing a key role in launching the *British Journal of Sociology* in 1949.

From 1949 to 1950 he served as the educational adviser to the British High Commission in Germany, and was appointed Martin White Professor of Sociology in 1954. From 1956 to 1960 he was the director of the social sciences department of UNESCO.

Marshall saw sociology as a discipline to be applied practically – hence his work in planning, education, and **equality**. He contributed to the development of social policy and administration through research that stretched from the nature of **citizenship** to a view of social welfare placed within the broader sociological context.

In 1950 he published *Citizenship and Social Class*,

which is a key text in both British sociology and the study of citizenship. His *Social Policy in the Twentieth Century* (1965) provides a clear analysis of the development of welfare policy from 1890, and he argued for the compatibility of modified capitalist enterprise and collectivist social policies, postulating that a free economic market contributed to the enhancement and creation of welfare.

Marshall continued to write after his retirement. Other publications include *Class, Citizenship, and Social Development* (1964) and *The Right to Welfare* (1981).

See also: **equality, citizenship, market**

Further reading: Bulmer and Rees 1996

Marx, Karl (1818–63) Born in Trier, and educated at the Universities of Bonn and Berlin. Originally a philosopher, Marx turned his attention to social questions as editor of the newspaper *Die Rheinische Zeitung*, in Cologne, but in 1843, the paper was banned by the Prussian authorities.

He wrote a detailed critique of **Hegel's** *Philosophy of Right*, and he began to argue that **emancipation** was not simply political but also social in character. Influenced by workers in Paris, he became a communist and worked with **Engels**, writing books that attacked left-wing supporters of **Hegel**.

In November 1847 he wrote *The Communist Manifesto*, and after the **revolutions** of 1848 he founded the *Neue Rheinische Zeitung*. But the revolutions of 1848 were all defeated and in 1849 Marx settled in Britain.

With only the money that Engels could raise, the Marx family lived in extreme poverty. He wrote important political analyses of struggles in France and then turned to his economic studies. He tried to raise money through articles (mostly written by Engels) for the *New York*

Daily Tribune. Before *Capital*, published in 1867, Marx had already drafted his *Introduction to the Critique of Political Economy* (known as the *Grundrisse*) and in 1859 he published *A Contribution to the Critique of Political Economy*, that contains his famous account of **historical materialism.**

He only became publicly known when as president of the First International, he expressed solidarity with the Paris Commune (which was brutally crushed after seventy-two days in office). After 1870 Marx became increasingly preoccupied with a struggle against the Russian anarchist **Bakunin,** and the International was transferred to New York where it died a natural death.

Capital was translated into Russian in 1872, and in 1875 Marx wrote a critique of the German socialist party programme accusing the latter of liberal formulas and abstractions.

See also: **Engels, Hegel, Bakunin**
Further reading: McLellan 2000

Marxism **Marx** famously declared that he was not a Marxist, and it is arguable that there is an inherent tension between his ideas and the movements that arose in his name.

Marx never saw a Marxist movement seize **power** during his lifetime. The **relationship** between Marx's theory and the movements he 'inspired', most notably the Russian **Revolution,** is highly contentious. There is evidence to suggest that Marx thought that socialist revolutions could only emancipate humanity if they took place in developed capitalist countries, and *Western Marxists* have held to this view, although without practical results.

Soviet Marxism used Marx's ideas to establish a highly authoritarian form of socialism that replicated itself after World War II in the Communist Party **states** of Eastern Europe. *Chinese Marxism* emphasised the importance of national independence, the centrality of will power and economic self-sufficiency, and *Cuban Marxism* arose out of the unwillingness of the USA to tolerate a left-leaning **nationalism**. It is certainly true that Marxism has been much more successful where it has been able to integrate itself with anti-colonial and anti-imperialist struggles in the so-called third world. In South Africa, Marxism has expressed itself through an independent Communist Party and even here it is closely integrated into a movement of national liberation.

Marxism as a political movement has usually been anti-liberal, with a problematic record on human rights. The exception is in Western Europe where the ideas of the Italian Marxist, **Gramsci**, led to a Marxism that emphasised the importance of winning popular consent and infusing Marxism with liberal values.

Although the prestige of Marxism has been severely dented by the collapse of many of the Communist Party states in 1989, the theory (in its many forms) continues to be influential throughout the world.

See also: **Marx, nationalism, Gramsci**
Further reading: McLellan 1979

Michels, Robert (1876–1936) Born in Cologne. He studied in England and at the Sorbonne.

He participated in the congress of the German Social Democratic Party (SDP) in 1903, 1904 and 1905, becoming a co-editor (with the support of **Weber**) of the *Archives of the Social Sciences and Politics*. He gained an academic position in Turin, and was greatly influenced by **syndicalism**.

In 1911 he published *Political Parties*. Here he argues that all societies and all organisations are subject to 'an iron law of oligarchy'. Struck by what he saw as the contrast between the official statements of the SDP and the timidity of its political practice, he argued that oligarchy is present even in parties apparently committed to the norms of **democracy**.

The fact that leaders are in practice autonomous from their followers derives from the constraints of organisation. Although he wrote a good deal about psychology, Michels argued that oligarchical tendencies are based upon organisational rather than psychological factors. The complexity of organisations can only be grasped by professional leaders who have communication skills, and who understand the rules of elections and other external pressures. This **leadership** is made all the more entrenched by what Michels regarded as the incompetence and emotional vulnerability of their mass membership.

In 1914 Michels wrote a study of Italian **imperialism** and published widely on **politics** and sociology. In 1930 he wrote the entry on 'Authority' for the *Encyclopaedia of the Social Sciences*. He admired **fascism** and argued that, as with Bolshevism, it was a reflection of the general tendency to oligarchy.

Michels also wrote a good deal on **nationalism**, with his later writings becoming increasingly anti-democratic in tone.

See also: **Weber, syndicalism, democracy, imperialism, fascism, nationalism**

Further reading: Beetham 1977

Miliband, Ralph (1924–94) Born in Brussels. His parents lived in the Jewish quarter in Warsaw.

In 1940, Miliband sailed to Britain, settling in London. He became a student, first at Acton Technical College, and then at the London School of Economics (LSE). He was active in left-wing groups and in 1943 became Vice President of the LSE Students' Union.

He was not only a committed Marxist, but also

greatly influenced by the radical socialist, Harold Laski. In 1943 he joined the Navy and saw action in the Mediterranean. He returned to the LSE and he wrote his doctoral thesis on the French **Revolution**. Having taught in Chicago, he acquired a teaching post at the LSE in 1949. Critical of **Stalin** and the foreign policy of the USSR, he became acquainted with left-wing members of the Labour Party, and worked with left-wing historians to launch *The New Reasoner* and the *New Left Review*. He later became an editor with Saville of the *Socialist Register*.

In 1961 he published a radical critique of the Labour Party, entitled *Parliamentary Socialism*, attacking the 'reformist' attachment to constitutional and parliamentary procedures. In the *Socialist Register* in 1967 he was fiercely critical of Harold Wilson for his pro-American stance over the Vietnam War.

In 1969 he wrote his widely read *The State in Capitalist Society* – a critique of pluralist views of **democracy** – and in 1977 he published *Marxism and Politics*, a work that sought to examine sympathetically the political theory of **Marxism**. *Capitalist Democracy in Britain* followed in 1982, and in 1983 a number of his key articles were reproduced in *Class Power and State Power*. He continued to address Marxist themes and his final book was *Socialism for a Sceptical Age*.

See also: **democracy**

Further reading: Newman 2004

Mill, James (1773–1836) Mill was ordained as a Presbyterian minister in 1798, but four years later gave up the **church** and became a journalist in London. He wrote for the *Edinburgh Review* and *St James Chronicle*.

He closely associated with **Bentham** and strongly supported the latter's theory of **utilitarianism**. He took upon himself the task of popularising Bentham's theories of law, **government**, education, psychology, and of course utility. He was an active member of the philosophical radicals, a group that came to include his own son, John Stuart **Mill**.

In 1817 he published his *History of British India*, a work that led to his position with the East India Company. In 1821 he published *Elements of Political Economy*, following Adam **Smith** in defending the **market** against mercantilism, and in 1829 he sought to furnish a psychological basis for utilitarianism in his *Analysis of the Phenomenon of the Mind*. His *Essay on Government* supported universal suffrage, but in a way that suggested that representative **government** could still be secured through a franchise that excluded women and the poor. He believed that the 'middle rank' or the middle classes would always be backed by the workers, although he was attacked by Macaulay for a deductive and what the latter considered to be an irresponsible defence of democratic rule.

See also: **Church, Bentham, utilitarianism, Mill, market**

Further reading: Fenn 1987

Mill, John Stuart (1806–73) Born in London, Mill was educated by his father, James **Mill** and **Bentham**. He had an extraordinary education and at 16 declared himself a utilitarian.

He was still young when he published articles in the *Westminister Review*, a journal founded to express the radical liberal position. However, at the age of 20, he suffered a nervous breakdown. He began to read poetry and nourish the world of feelings that he felt had been neglected in his upbringing. He was influenced by **Saint-Simon** and Carlyle, and struck up a friendship with Harriet Taylor (whom he eventually married).

In 1823 he began work for the East India office, and in 1834 founded with William Molesworth the *London Review*. Mill was greatly influenced by Tocqueville, and in 1843 he published *System of Logic*. In 1848 his *Principles of Political Economy* followed, and in the later editions Mill became more and more explicitly hostile to free-**market capitalism**. In 1859 he wrote his highly influential *On Liberty*, a work that breaks new ground by concerning itself not merely with the physical force of the law, but what Mill called the 'moral **coercion**' of public opinion.

In *Considerations of Representative Government* that appeared in 1861, Mill advocated proportional **representation** and plural voting as ways of trying to neutralise working-class influence, and in the same year, he brought out his work on *Utilitarianism* where he sought to defend a revised version of the Benthamite doctrine. *The Subjection of Women* that appeared in 1869 is a courageous exposition of liberal **feminism**.

He was elected to parliament in 1865 and he sought unsuccessfully to amend the 1873 Reform Act so as to secure votes for women.

See also: **Mill, James, Bentham, Saint-Simon, Tocqueville, capitalism, coercion, feminism**

Further reading: Ryan 1974

Millett, Kate (1934–) Born in St Paul, Minnesota. She graduated from the University of Minnesota in 1956 and studied at Oxford. She worked as a teacher and sculptor, living in New York and Japan, before working on her Ph.D. at Columbia. She wrote a manifesto on sexual **politics** for the first Women's Liberation group at Columbia in 1968.

Her thesis was published as *Sexual Politics* in 1970 and here she focussed on Mailer, Miller, Lawrence and Genet, arguing that **power**, not eroticism, was their real subject, and that they were concerned to justify male domination in sexual encounters. She provided a historical account of the rise of **feminism,** and she extolled novels like Brontë's *Villette* for the way they explored the problems of women looking beyond a patriarchal order.

She broadened the notion of **politics** so that the apparently '**natural' relationship** between the sexes could be seen as political because it involved power, and she extended the concept of **patriarchy** to embrace male domination – a social structural attribute and not a biological one. Her arguments had a seminal impact on the development of second-wave feminism. She emphasised the importance of socialisation in generating patriarchy, and contended that its values were inherent in formal education, popular culture, religion, and art. She was particularly hostile to **Freud,** seeing his theory of psychoanalysis as a justification for women's subordination.

She chaired the New York education committee of the US National Organization of Women. *Flying* (1974) and *Sita* (1977) were published as autobiographical accounts exploring her own sexuality, while *Going to Iran* (1981) recalls her attempts to assist in the struggle for women's **rights** in Iran. She was expelled from the country by the Khomeini **government.**

See also: **feminism, politics, natural, patriarchy**
Further reading: Millett 1977

Mills, C(harles) Wright (1916–62) Born in Waco, Texas. He received his Ph.D. from the University of Wisconsin where he came into contact with Gerth who introduced Mills to **Marx, Weber** and the Frankfurt School.

In 1941 he acquired a post at the University of Maryland, and vigorously opposed the Second World War. He saw himself as an American progressive rather than a Marxist, and supported the journal *Politics* where he analysed the way in which war and **conflict** engineered a consensual acceptance of domination. In his *The New Men of Power* he examined the **power** of union leaders over their followers.

Mills obtained a position at the Columbia University in 1946 and he and Gerth published *Character and Social Structure* in 1953. However, his reputation was made by two books, *White Collar: the American Middle Classes* (1951) and *The Power Elite* (1956). In *White Collar* he argues that the 'new middle classes' were 'cheerful robots' who would support the right rather than the left. In the *Power Elite* he talked about the concentration of power by an elite consisting of political, industrial and military leaders. This undermined **democracy** and created the climate for war. The 'high and mighty' maintained close social cohesion through intermarriage and socialising.

However, he became more optimistic in the 1950s, and *The Causes of World War Three* presented critical intellectuals as agents of change. In *Listen Yankee* he defended the Cuban **Revolution**, and in *The Sociological Imagination* and *The Marxists* he argued the case for a new leftism composed of radical and youthful intellectuals.

See also: **Marx, Weber, power, democracy**
Further reading: Tilman 1984

momentum concept This is a concept that is capable of being reconstructed in a progressive and egalitarian way.

Tocqueville defined **democracy** as a concept that was continuously moving, so that at one time it was anti-feudal, and then it could be interpreted as being anti-capitalist.

Momentum concepts like **freedom, equality** and **emancipation** have a logic to them that is egalitarian whereas concepts like the **state**, violence and **division** can be called static because they necessarily exclude some and privilege others.

Momentum concepts are likely to be feared by conservatives on the grounds that they can always be interpreted to urge further change. It would wrong to think that a momentum concept can ever be finally 'realised' since by definition there is always more to come.

See also: **Tocqueville, freedom, equality, emancipation, state**

Further reading: Hoffman 2001

Montesquieu, Charles-Louis (1689–1755) Born in Bordeaux, France. He studied science and history at school and became a lawyer in local **government**.

In 1721 he published *The Persian Letters*. In this work **politics**, morals and love are skilfully woven together, and a critique is presented of religion and **Aristotle**. He was elected to the French Academy of Science in 1728, and in 1730 was elected to the Royal Society in London.

Two years later, he published his *Considerations on the Causes of the Greatness of the Romans and Their Decline*. Here he tackled **Machiavelli**'s notion of *virtu* (a concept that attacked Aristotelian and Christian views), and he saw in ancient Rome problems to which all republics are prone.

His greatest work is *On the Spirit of Laws* (1848). All human activity, he contended, is governed by laws, whether social or **natural**, and he regarded the natural condition as one from which humans need to escape. Positive laws can only maintain peace and security if they avoid terror, and despotism is seen as an illegitimate form of rule. But whether the **state** is a republic or monarchy depends upon circumstances – the historical and geographical environment. This creates the 'spirit' of the nation. The best **government** is a balance with a king, a parliament, and a judiciary. Virtue of a Machiavellian kind is desirable but it can be inimical to individuality. The English Constitution is extolled for attaining a 'balance' allowing commerce and security, and he presented a somewhat idealised version of the 'separation of powers'.

Like many of his day, Montesquieu condoned **slavery** and regarded women as unsuitable either to head households or rule over others.

See also: **politics, Aristotle, Machiavelli, natural, government, slavery**

Further reading: Richter 1977

morality A term that refers to injunctions of what to do, and how to behave, in particular circumstances.

Political morality becomes problematic when focussed upon the **state**. It could be argued that it is difficult to see how the state can act morally when its distinctive attribute is the use of **force** to tackle conflicts of interest. The 'morality' of the state is of a distinctively propagandist quality, designed to bully and coerce people into compliance.

Morality is sometimes seen as norms that are imposed from on high. This is the negation of morality since people who abide by norms out of fear of the consequences, or as a result of lack of knowledge of the alternatives, cannot be said to act morally. Morality implies an **autonomy** and a willingness to criticise so that the 'moral' injunctions associated with authoritarian rule – whether of a personal or institutional kind – undermine rather than further morality.

The attempt to present **politics** as a science devoid of moral or normative implications is misguided. Science itself, whether natural or social, has moral implications, and the notion that factual statements must be morally neutral fails to understand that values derive from statements that could only be considered meaningful if they postulate **relationships**. Thus, for example, a statement about apathy, for example, cannot but postulate some kind of relationship between apathy and a political system, and it is in this relationship that we find value judgements. Hence morality is inherent in **politics**, since politics is concerned with **relationships** that result in **conflict**.

See also: **state, force, autonomy, relationship, politics, conflict**

Further reading: Jordan 1989

Mosca, Gaetano (1858–1941) He taught constitutional law at the University of Palmero between 1858 and 1888, and at the Universities of Rome and Turin. He was a member of the Chamber of Deputies in 1908, Under-secretary of State for the colonies between 1914 and 1916 and made a senator for life in 1919.

In 1884 he published *Theory of Governments and Parliamentary Government,* but is best known for his *The Ruling Class,* that appeared in 1896. All societies, he argued, are governed by minorities whether these are military, hereditary, priestly or based on merit or wealth. He accepted that ownership could be a factor in accounting for elite rule, but he rejected the Marxist account on the grounds that it seeks to privilege this particular factor. The ruling **class** or elite owes its superiority to organisational factors, he argued, and its skills alter according to circumstance. What he called the 'political formula' or the ideological mechanisms of rule varied, but whatever the form, all **states** are necessarily elitist in character, whether their legitimating myth is the divine right of kings, popular **sovereignty** or the dictatorship of the proletariat. **Democracy**, in his view, was a simply a more subtle form of manipulation, and the parties offered inducements for people to vote for them. The 'political class' needed to be distinguished from other sections of the elite, like industrialists, but in 1923 he introduced in his work the argument that elites could compete through rival political parties. People of lower socio-economic origin can be recruited in order to renew elites. Unlike other elitists, he was fiercely critical of Mussolini, and his theory can be regarded as an early version of the 'democratic **elitism**' expounded by **Schumpeter** and **Dahl**.

See also: **Schumpeter, Dahl**

Further reading: Albertoni 1987

multi-culturalism A term that recognises the reality of contemporary liberal societies today, in which people exist within communities with many faiths, various ethnicities and diverse cultures.

Multi-culturalism implies not merely a recognition of this diversity, but also an acknowledgement that this diversity is positive and empowering. Each group strengthens the other by drawing upon different values and traditions, so that its own identity is in a process of continual change.

Multi-culturalism implies **toleration** but toleration seen as an attitude that is active, and not simply passive. Multi-culturalism is, it could be argued, in tension with the institution of the **state**, since it opposes the idea that there is a dominant culture. Diversity cannot be celebrated if one culture is placed in a position of privilege over others.

Multi-culturalism must be based upon **emancipation**. Traditions that are divisive and undemocratic are problematic so that multi-culturalism is discredited if it becomes a kind of relativism that regards all cultural practices as valid simply because they take place.

Underpinning multi-culturalism is a commitment to **democracy** since cultural practices cannot be empowering if they conflict with democracy and create tension and division.

See also: **toleration, state, emancipation, democracy**
Further reading: Parekh 2000

N

nationalism It is generally agreed that nationalism can be ideologically ambiguous, so that nationalists can be right wing, left wing or somewhere in between. What unites all nationalists, however, is a belief that loyalty to the nation is the highest political attribute that an individual or group can adopt.

How old is nationalism? Some see it as a relatively recent phenomenon, arising from the French **Revolution**, while others trace it back to tribal formations, arguing that the roots of nationalism lie in the ethnic particularity of a given group. There is a close link between nationalism and the **state**. State functionaries necessarily make a claim to exercise a monopoly of legitimate **force**, and the cultural expression this takes expresses itself as nationalism.

Nationalism needs to be distinguished from national identity. The latter is a necessary, but not a sufficient, condition for nationalism since nationalists privilege one particular national identity above all others, whereas it is quite possible for a person to have a number of national identities, along with an infinite number of other identities as well. This is why there is a logical tension between creeds like **liberalism** and socialism that profess universal aspirations, and nationalism that privileges one identity over others.

See also: **state**
Further reading: Hutchinson and Smith 1994

natural Something is natural if it develops humans or other organisms. Thus it can be said that living in a family is 'natural' because it enables humans, for example, to flourish.

The concept is, however, often used pejoratively by political theorists. The term 'naturalism' points to the use of the use of the term 'nature' to denote something that is static and unchangeable. Thus the notion that all men are breadwinners, while women should work in the home, can be said to 'naturalise' social **relationships**, that is, ignore their dynamic and fluid quality.

Pre-liberal thought regards the natural as denoting repressive **hierarchy** and static differentiation, so that **slavery** is seen as natural and so is the **state**. The liberal tradition uses the term in an egalitarian way so that humans are seen as naturally free and equal with a natural inclination to govern their own lives. The problem, it could be argued, is that although this notion of the natural is preferable to pre-liberal usages, it is still static, and presupposes that nature is externally created.

Once we hold that nature creates itself, then the term natural changes dramatically. It can no longer be said that what is natural is unchangeable, since nature itself continually changes, albeit on an evolutionary time scale. Humans are part of nature, and have evolved from nature. Their relationship to nature is clearly an active one, and nature has been radically transformed as a result of human intervention. This affects both people and the environment in which they live, and it is a major challenge facing humanity that they alter nature in positive ways.

The development of nature is necessarily linked to the development of humans: their well-being and preservation are intrinsically linked. What is natural is, therefore, what is developmental, so that the term indicates both a continuity with the past as well as a process of transformation.

See also: **slavery, state**

Further reading: Collingwood 1949

New Left A group of socialist thinkers, like Perry Anderson or Robin Blackburn, radical but hostile to the Communist Party **states**, who became influential from the 1950s.

Although they differed among themselves, all rejected what they saw as the 'reformism' of the Labour Party and the 'Stalinism' of the Communist Parties. They considered the socialism of Eastern Europe to be an 'anti-model', and felt that socialism must respect freedom of thought.

Often influenced by **anarchism,** the New Left were critical of parties in general, fearing that they would limit the critical independence of intellectuals. They were opposed to 'orthodox **Marxism**', and felt that Marxism itself must be open to debate. New theories should be encouraged, and journals were produced that presented arguments in a critical and sophisticated way.

The New Left interpreted **politics** in a broad sense, so that questions of psychology and aesthetics could be expounded and analysed alongside more conventional political questions.

They remain an influential current within the socialist and radical movement

See also: **Marxism, politics**

Further reading: Long 1969

New Right A group of radical thinkers in the 1970s and 1980s, like the economist **Hayek** (who was knighted by Thatcher) or the politician Keith Joseph, who were hostile to the 'consensus' politics of social democrats, new liberals and reformist conservatives.

The New Right championed the idea of the free **market** and some (like **Rothbard**) even espoused a form of **anarchism**. They were strongly opposed to **state** intervention for welfare purposes, but they divided over whether individuals should be wholly 'free' even if this meant engaging in acts of self-destruction, like taking hard drugs.

Although they were seen as resurrecting classical **liberalism**, it is important to note that they saw liberty, but not **equality**, as a guiding virtue.

See also: **liberalism**, **equality**

Further reading: Levitas 1986

new social movements These are movements that sprang up in the 1960s, and they embrace single issues like **feminism**, the environment, **animal rights**, peace, and so on.

They are considered to be *social* movements because they support a broad view of **politics**, emphasising the importance of personal development in a collective context. They are *new* because they are sceptical of conventional views of politics, regarding the **state** with suspicion.

The adherents of new social movements (NSMs) are often influenced by individual aspects of anarchist theory (rather than **anarchism** as a whole). They are strongly anti-authoritarian and hostile to dogmas and 'closed' ideologies.

The theory suffers from the dilemmas of classical anarchism, since in practice NSMs have to direct themselves to the state and existing political parties in order to be effective. They are best seen as movements that enrich the existing political process rather than constitute an alternative to it.

NSMs have an emancipatory content. Hence they are

narrower than mere pressure groups, since they consciously seek to challenge conventional **relationships** and hierarchies.

See also: **feminism, animal rights, politics, state, anarchism**

Further reading: Maheu 1995

Nietzsche, Friedrich (1844–1900) Born in Prussia. In 1864 he became a student of theology and philology at the University of Bonn, and in the following year continued his studies at the University of Leipzig. In 1869 was appointed professor of classical philology at the University of Basel.

In 1870 he served as a medical orderly in the Franco-Prussian war, and two years later he published *The Birth of Tragedy* where he argued that tragedy played a central role for the ancient Greeks in maintaining their certainty about life. The book was dedicated to the composer Richard Wagner, and called into question much of the received wisdom about ancient Greece.

However he broke with Wagner, and in 1879 he resigned from the University. He spent the next ten years in southern Switzerland and northern Italy, and in 1883 he began work on *Thus Spoke Zarathustra*. In 1886 he wrote *Beyond Good and Evil*, and a year later he published *On the Genealogy of Morals*. His argument in the latter centres on the moralities of slave and master, and he regards the triumph of slave **morality** as the internalisation of oppression. In 1888 he wrote *Ecce Homo*, a work that was published posthumously in April 1908.

He became insane in 1889 and spent the last eleven years of his life in the care of his mother and sister. Although the Nazis made use of his work, their support was misleading since Nietzsche opposed **nationalism** as a futile attempt to prevent the disintegration of the modern state. He anticipated the First World War as a war 'such as no-one has ever seen'.

His work has enjoyed a recent revival particularly among some postmodernists who like Nietzsche's critique of **liberalism** and the Enlightenment.

See also: **nationalism, state**

Further reading: Ansell-Pearson 1994

Nozick, Robert (1938–2002) Born and educated in Brooklyn. He joined the Socialist Party in his youth, and as an undergraduate at the Columbia University he founded a local branch of the Student League for Industrial Democracy.

While a graduate student at Princeton, he became convinced by arguments in favour of **capitalism** and became a professor at Harvard in 1969. In 1974 he published his famous *Anarchy, State and Utopia* in which he argued that individual **rights** in the Lockean tradition are primary, and that **state** intervention should be limited to the enforcement of contracts, and protection against violence and theft. He took the view that his minimal state could be established on anarchist principles. The work was hugely influential and was widely seen as providing a philosophical justification for the **New Right**.

Between 1981 and 1984 he was chair of the philosophy department at Harvard. In 1981 he published *Philosophical Explanations* – a work that tackled questions of identity, free will, ethics and a theory of knowledge in terms of a philosophical **pluralism**. This acknowledged that various philosophical views could all be sincerely held and plausible even if they are mutually incompatible.

In 1989 he published *The Examined Life*, and four years later, *The Nature of Rationality*, a work that looked at the nature of decisions. He taught in a variety of departments, and his final book was entitled *Invariances:*

the Structure of the Objective World (2001). He held many distinctions and although he and **Rawls** had very different positions, they cooperated with other philosophers in arguing that the Supreme Court should allow mentally competent, terminally ill patients to commit assisted suicide.

See also: **capitalism, state, New Right, Rawls**
Further reading: Corlett 1991

O

Oakeshott, Michael (1901–90) Born in Kent. He was a student at Cambridge in 1920, where he became a fellow in 1925.

In 1933 he published *Experience and its Modes*. Here he spoke of three standpoints or 'modes', practice, science and history (Oakeshott later added poetry), each being unique, self-contained and inevitably limited. Practice was the mode that stresses willing and doing; science emphasised the importance of quantity; and history focussed on pastness. Philosophy by contrast sought coherence and rigour, aiming at experience as a whole.

Oakeshott was becoming more and more concerned with political philosophy, and published work on **Hobbes**. In 1939 he published *The Social and Political Doctrines of Contemporary Europe*. During the Second World War, he served in Intelligence, and after the war he returned to Cambridge. In 1951 he acquired a chair in **politics** at the London School of Economics.

In 1962 *Rationalism in Politics* appeared. **Politics**, he argued, involves seeking to attend to problems in a way that avoids the narrowness of **empiricism** and the abstractness of rationalism. Both empiricism and rationalism neglect the importance of tradition.

In 1975 he published *On Human Conduct*. Here he argued that political or civil philosophy is concerned to analyse human conduct in terms of its practices. These practices are either instrumental or moral (that is, non-instrumental). A civil (or political) association is moral and governed by law: this enables people to get on with their life as they fit. Notions of distributive **justice** or programmes of reform get in the way of a civil association, and are instrumental in character.

His final book *History and Other Essays* appeared in 1983. He had reluctantly accepted honorary doctorates at Durham and Colerado and he became a fellow of the British Academy in 1966.

See also: **Hobbes, politics**

Further reading: Greenleaf 1965

obligation A general term that relates to obedience to laws, norms and rules.

In pre-liberal thought obligation is seen as **natural**. Obligation is a passive and unconditional response born of the fact that people find themselves in particular hierarchical **relationships** in which they are obligated to their superior.

Liberalism introduces the all-important notion of will. Obligation relates to those laws that have been authorised by the citizen. Of course, conditional obligation only applies historically to a small elite, and most of society – women, the poor, the youth, and so on. – have to obey their designated superiors. Nevertheless, the notion that obligation must be tied to **consent** is an important concept, and is capable of wider application as excluded groups campaign for **emancipation**.

Obligation to the **state**, it could be argued, is problematic, since the use or credible threat of **force** cannot engender obligation. Obedience to the state becomes a tactical question. Do I choose to obey laws based on force simply because the consequence of disobedience is highly inconvenient, or because the laws encapsulate moral norms that I would follow anyway?

Obligation is more than a mere duty. Obligation is a compulsory act, whereas duty is something that is desirable. I have a duty to help the infirm across a busy road, but do I have an obligation to do so? Obligations are 'binding' in a way, arguably, that duties are not.

Obligations are based on development. An obligation to one's own or another's well-being derives from the fact that personal and social development is impossible without it. Obligation is voluntary in the sense that it must be consciously willed. But it is involuntary because it is a commitment that has to be fulfilled, or sanctions will necessarily follow.

See also: **natural, relationship, liberalism, consent, emancipation, state, force**

Further reading: Pateman 1985

Ontology A concept that simply refers to a theory of being. Usually contrasted with epistemology as a theory of knowledge.

An ontological view of the **state**, for example, poses the question: does the state actually exist? Being needs to be kept separate from knowledge, since we cannot speak of ideas as a reflection of the material world, if we confuse them.

A materalist would argue that ideas are ontologically part of matter since they are the product of a brain, itself a material organ. Epistmologically, however, ideas can be judged true or false depending upon how accurately they reflect the material world.

Further reading: Yolton 2000

Orwell, George (1903–50) Born in Motohari, India. Educated at Eton and in 1922 he joined the Indian Imperial Police in Burma.

In 1933 he wrote *Down and Out in Paris and London* where he recalled his life as a dishwasher and a tramp. The work was eventually accepted by the publishers, Gollancz. Here he abandoned his birth name 'Eric Blair'. A year later he wrote *Burmese Days*. Three novels followed in the 1930s – *A Clergyman's Daughter* (1935), *Keep the Aspidistra Flying* (1936) and *Coming Up for Air* (1939).

In 1937 he published *The Road to Wigan Pier* in which he examines the lives of miners in Wigan. In 1938 *Homage to Catalonia* appeared. Here Orwell recalled his engagement in the Spanish civil war, the conditions of fighting (he supported POUM, a radical Marxist grouping that was anarchist aligned), – how he got wounded and the problems with the Communists. He had been hugely impressed by the lack of **class** distinctions and the general social **equality** in Barcelona, but after being wounded at the front he returned to Barcelona, only to be hounded by the Communists. With the help of the British consul, he escaped to France.

His two most famous books followed in the 1940s. In 1945 he wrote *Animal Farm*, a witty critique of Stalinism and the Russian **Revolution**, and *Nineteen Eighty-Four*, in which he depicted life under an authoritarian regime that was presented as a dystopia. Declared unfit to fight, he worked for the BBC during the war (the results were published in *George Orwell: the Lost Writings* and *The War Commentaries*).

His celebrated essay *Politics and the English Language*, published in 1950, has been particularly influential.

Further reading: Crick 1980

Owen, Robert (1771–1858) Born in Newtown in Wales. After business experience in Stamford and Manchester, Owen purchased textile factories in New Lanark in Scotland, where he sought to create a new type of **community**. He believed passionately that a person's character is formed by the effects of their environment.

He laid much stress upon educating young people and in 1813 he wrote *The Formation of Character*. The following year, he published *A New View of Society*, where he argued that religion, marriage and private **property** are barriers to progress. In 1815 Owen sent detailed proposals to Parliament about his ideas on factory reform, and appeared before Peel and his Commons committee in 1816.

He saw himself creating a new moral world, a world from which the bitterness of divisive sectarian religion would be banished. Disappointed with the response his ideas received in Britain, Owen purchased an area of Indiana, USA for £30,000 and called the community he established there New Harmony.

By 1827 Owen had sold his New Lanark textile mills, and he devoted his energies to trying to obtain factory reform, adult suffrage and the development of successful trade unions.

Owen played an important role in establishing the Grand National Consolidated Trade Union in 1834 and the Association of All Classes and All Nations in 1835. He also attempted to form a new community, at East Tytherly in Hampshire. However, like New Harmony in America, this experiment came to an end after disputes between members of the community.

See also: **property**
Further reading: Morton 1969

P

Paine, Thomas (1737–1809) Born in Norfolk. He was educated at the local grammar school in Thetford, and after learning various trades, he became a school teacher in London.

In 1768 he went to Lewes and set up a local debating club. Working as an excise officer, he wrote a pamphlet urging higher wages for excisemen, as a result of which he was dismissed. Meeting Franklin, he decided to emigrate to the United States.

He acquired employment on a journal in Pennsylvania, and in 1776 he published *Common Sense*. Here he argued for American independence, and he was involved with drawing up a liberal **state** constitution for Pennsylvania. During the war of independence he fought in Washington's army

In 1781 he visited Europe, seeking to raise money for the American cause. In 1791 he published *The Rights of Man* in which he attacked hereditary and monarchical systems, and argued for popular **sovereignty** and equal individual **rights**. His work attacked **Burke** (to whom Paine's views were a particular anathema), and along with political changes (including the abolition of the House of Lords) he urged social reforms in terms of progressive taxation and welfare measures.

Paine's book was banned and the British **government** prosecuted for seditious libel. Nevertheless, the book was widely read, and Paine escaped to France where he became a French citizen and was elected to the National Convention. He argued against the execution of the king (although Paine was a passionate republican), was imprisoned and narrowly escaped execution himself. After his release he published *The Age of Reason* where he produced an attack on established religion including a critique of the Old Testament and the Gospels, and this extended his notoriety to the United States itself.

In 1796 he published *Agrarian Justice* and returned to America in 1802.

See also: **Burke**

Further reading: Williamson 1973

Pareto, Vilfredo (1848–1923) Born in the year of the European **revolutions**. He trained as an engineer, and followed J. S. **Mill** and Spencer in supporting parliamentary reform and the free-**market** economy. He was intensely critical of the way in which industrialists used the **state** for their own ends

He initially backed the liberals and acquired a formidable reputation as an economist. He took the chair in political economy at the University of Lausanne in 1894, publishing his *Cours d'économie politique* (1896, 1897). In 1900 he declared himself an anti-democrat, arguing that the political movements in Italy and France were simply seeking to replace one elite with another. While he approved of **Marx**'s emphasis upon struggle, he rejected completely the notion that a classless society was possible

In 1906, Pareto published his *Manual of Political Economy*, where he presented pure economics in mathematical form. **Croce** convinced him that 'rational economic man' did not correspond to reality. Human action is mostly non-logical in character, he argued, and stems from non-rational sentiments and impulses: what Pareto called underlying 'residues'. In his most important political and sociological work, the *Mind and Society* that he wrote in 1916, he distinguishes between Class I residues, inventive, imaginative capacities, and Class II residues, conservative, persistent tendencies.

All **government** is government by an elite who use a

combination of **coercion** and **consent**. Class I residues predominate when 'foxes' are in control – manipulative politicians who create consent – and Class II residues when violence is necessary. Each of these residues has its strengths and weaknesses, and the 'circulation of elites' can be explained as 'lions' – those who rule through brute force – replace 'foxes'. He saw in Mussolini a politician with a lion-like character who had displaced wily politicians.

See also: **Mill**

Further reading: Bobbio 1972

Pateman, Carole (1940–) Born in Sussex. She attended her local girls' grammar school but left at 16.

She went to adult-education Ruskin College in 1963 and then went on to Oxford University, where she obtained her Ph D.

She has taught and researched in Europe, Australia, and North America. In 1970 she published *Participation and Democratic Theory*, a radical work that examines sympathetically the experience of workers' control. *The Problem of Political Obligation: A Critical Analysis of Liberal Theory* followed in 1979. This argues that liberal theory is inconsistent in that it combines a belief in the **force** of the **state** with an emphasis on the **freedom** of the individual. In the late 1970s she began to develop an interest in the link between **feminism** and political theory, and published a number of articles that were critical of **liberalism** as a patriarchal theory.

Her work *The Sexual Contract* that came out in 1988 made a major impact upon feminist political theory, and established Pateman as a leading figure in this area.

The Disorder of Women: Democracy, Feminism, and

Political Theory followed in 1989. This offered, among other things, a feminist critique of the welfare state. *Feminist Interpretations and Political Theory* that she co-edited with M. Shanley in 1991 contains a brilliant analysis of the patriarchal assumptions of **Hobbes**.

Pateman was President of the Australasian Political Science Association. She served on the Council of the American Political Science Association, and was the first woman President of the International Political Science Association, holding the post from 1991 to 1994. She was elected as a Fellow of the American Academy of Arts and Sciences in 1996. She currently teaches in the Department of Political Science at the University of California at Los Angeles.

See also: **feminism, force, state, freedom, liberalism, Hobbes**

Further reading: Pateman 1981

patriarchy A term that initially referred to the **power** of fathers over sons, but was later extended to embrace male domination in general. When it first appeared, it was linked to the anti-liberal view of **hierarchy** and the **state** as institutions that were **natural**.

Patriarchalism in the seventeenth century was employed to defend absolutism and the divine right of kings, and challenge the liberal doctrine of the state of nature and the **social contract**. Sir Robert Filmer (1588–1653) was explicitly attacked by **Locke** on this score.

The term has been dramatically broadened under feminist scholarship. Patriarchy is seen as male domination in general – over women, children, and the world of nature. Feminists divide over whether patriarchy is inherent in men, or whether it constitutes a set of values that a few women might also adopt and (a few) men might challenge and reject. Is patriarchy a system or **structure** that people unwittingly adopt, or should we see it as the conscious result of a pursuit of privilege and power?

There is further controversy as to whether patriarchy is necessarily private or whether it can take a public, institutional form. The notion is accompanied by a broad view of the political process, so that male chauvinism in inter-personal relations can be deemed patriarchal in character. The welfare state is sometimes seen as public patriarchy – an institution that pursues discriminatory policies against women – and the state itself is seen as patriarchal. Opinion divides as to whether the state is inherently patriarchal, or merely contingently so. Much hinges on the analysis of violence. If violence is deemed essentially patriarchal in character, then it is difficult to see how the state itself can avoid being patriarchal as an institution that uses **force** to settle conflicts of interest.

See also: **hierarchy, state, natural, social contract, Locke, feminism, state, force**

Further reading: Beechey 1979

Plato (427–347 BC) Born into an aristocratic family. He became friends with Socrates during his youth.

Plato fought for the Athenians between 409 and 404 BC but after the execution of Socrates, he decided to have nothing more to do with **politics**. He travelled widely and in Italy he was greatly influenced by the work of Pythagoras. In 387 BC he founded his Academy in Athens where he hoped to train statesmen and women.

He went to Syracuse in 367 BC, but failed to provide a settlement to the political rivalries there.

He is famous for his contributions in philosophy, mathematics and science. His dialogues invariably have

Socrates as the major figure and he discusses a wide range of topics.

In *The Republic* Plato seeks to establish a just society as an ideal, rooted in a '**natural**' division of labour. Its rulers are 'guardians' who live a communal life – without private **property**, family or personal ambition. Significantly, Plato allows women to be guardians although the explicitly elitist character of his **state** means that he is not regarded as a feminist.

Like the state, the individual is just when an impartial reason governs turbulent emotions, and **force** is to be used if the lower orders fail to see the timeless values of the common good.

In the *Statesman* he acknowledges that until philosophers have been trained, a more conventional polity is required, arguing for monarchy provided the state abides by its laws. In *Laws* (his final work) the wise form a Nocturnal Council, and since this polity is less 'ideal', people do have some legal **rights** against their rulers. He now relies more upon history than the contemplative speculation of *The Republic*.

See also: **natural, property, state, force**

Further reading: Mieksins Wood and Wood 1978

Plekhanov, Georgi (1856–1918) Born in Gudalovka, Russia. He joined Land and Freedom and was the main speaker and organiser at a demonstration in St Petersburg in 1876.

A supporter of the anti-terrorist wing the populists, he was forced into exile in 1880, settling in Geneva. Here he helped to form the Liberation of Labour group and cemented Marxist argumentation in his *Socialism and the Political Struggle* (1893) and *Our Differences* (1895). The **revolution** would be initially 'bourgeois' in character, but the Russian bourgeoisie were seen as too timid to carry through this revolution Ironically, therefore, the proletariat had to lead such a revolution.

He published under the pseudonym of 'Beltov' the *Monist View of History* where he expounds and defends **dialectical** and **historical materialism**, drawing heavily upon the work of **Engels**. He wrote a number of books developing these arguments, and they became classics of Marxist instruction. **Lenin** was greatly influenced by Plekhanov's style and content.

He was a founder member of the Russian Social Democratic Labour Party in 1898 and one of the editors of *Iskra* two years later. He sided with Lenin and the Bolsheviks when the party split in 1903, but soon joined the Mensheviks, likening Lenin to Robespierre – a leader with highly authoritarian tendencies.

He was unenthusiastic in his support for the 1905 revolution. In 1912 he wrote *Art and Social Life* where he links art to the prevalence of **class** values. He supported the Russian **state** in the First World War, arguing that the defeat of Germany was in the interests of international socialism, and after Tsarism collapsed in 1917, he returned to Russia to support the Provisional Government.

See also: **revolution, dialectics, historical materialism, Engels, Lenin**

Further reading: Baron 1963

pluralism Pluralism stands as a protest against 'monism' or one-ness, and emphasises that **difference** and multiplicity must be taken seriously.

Pluralism is sometimes identified with the argument that in a liberal **democracy, interests** are diverse so that it is wrong to regard one factor – such as wealth, popularity, ethnicity – as ultimately predominant. This doctrine became discredited in the late 1960s and during the

1970s, since it was felt that the notion that in liberal societies different groups 'balanced' themselves out was propagandistic and inaccurate.

More recently, critiques of the liberal pluralism of the 1960s have themselves been criticised on the grounds that an emphasis upon underlying **structures** that unify society generates dogmatism, exclusivity and authoritarianism. Why – it has been argued against radical **feminism** – should plurality 'stop' with the acknowledgement that individuals can be either male or female?

The **postmodernist** argument enshrines pluralism as its key value. Thus postmodern feminism argues that not only are women different to men, but they are also different to one another. An infinite range of other factors needs to be taken into account – a person's **class**, religion, language, culture, region, and so on. The search for the 'truth' or a belief in 'reason' represent 'monist' postures that must be challenged and rejected.

The problem with pluralism is that it can operate its own system of 'privileging', so that differences are seen as more important than similarities. If women differ among themselves, does this mean that feminism itself is impossible since the whole notion of women has been dethroned?

Pluralism can only be sustained as an outlook and approach if it operates alongside, and does not exclude, a stress upon sameness. Difference and diversity are important, but they need to be linked to universality – what things have in common.

See also: **difference, feminism, postmodernism**
Further reading: McLennan 1995

political correctness A term that is increasingly used pejoratively, but which denotes an attitude that supports **emancipation** and self-development.

Political correctness (PC) is usually associated with anti-racism and **feminism** where 'politically correct' attitudes are those that seek to advance **equality** for all individuals, and show sensitivity to the problems facing women. However, the term can apply more generally to take account of the sensitivities of people from the so-called 'third world'.

Under the impact of **globalisation** and **multiculturalism,** we live in a world in which people are conscious of **difference** and see the importance of celebrating rather than denigrating these differences.

PC has made a particularly significant impact upon North American universities and, like many new ideas, it is sometimes presented in an 'extremist' and unattractive way. This has enabled conservatives in particular to discredit PC as being doctrinaire and intolerant whereas in fact PC seeks emancipation and a positive attitude to life. It is important that a good cause is not spoiled through zealotry, and a humorous and relaxed view of the world is central to support for egalitarianism.

We should perhaps (as a way round this problem) distinguish between PC and pseudo-PC, regarding the latter as an arrogant and insecure attempt to implement the real thing.

See also: **feminism, equality, globalisation, multiculturalism, difference**

Further reading: Dunant 1994

politics Politics involves the resolution of **conflict**. The term has, however, been traditionally defined in terms of the **state,** although more recently broader social conceptions have been embraced.

The statist concept runs into the problem of how to define activity that occurs independently of the state. Do stateless societies, domestic or international, lack politics?

Behaviouralists conceive of politics as a system that exists at various levels. But the difficulty with this kind of definition is that it simply ignores the state.

Paradoxically, it could be argued that there is an inverse relation between politics and the state. Where the state intervenes, there politics comes to an end, an argument recognised in the argument, for example, that a conflict like the Northern Ireland one needs to be resolved politically rather than militarily. Here the term 'politics' is used to denote the absence of organised **force**.

Human society will always generate conflict, since conflict is rooted in the differences between individuals and groups. However this conflict does not necessarily involve violence, and where it does not, such conflict can be resolved through politics. Politics is the resolution of conflicts, and must involve compromise, negotiation and arbitration. Where force is involved, then it is impossible to actually resolve conflicts (they can only be suppressed or contained), so that politics, unlike the state, is a process of resolving conflict, and this can only be done in a way that leaves the subjective status of parties to a dispute in tact.

Politics is inherent in society and is a public activity. Where **relationships** do not involve conflict, or this conflict is purely embryonic, politics is not present. But in a more or less formal sense, it is difficult to avoid for any length of time.

See also: **conflict, state, behaviouralism, force, relationship**

Further reading: Leftwich 1984

Popper, Karl (1902–94) Born in Vienna. He left Austria just before the Nazi *Anschluss*.

In 1934 he published *The Logic of Scientific Discovery*

where he argued that ideas have to be falsified rather than verified. He taught philosophy in New Zealand from 1937 to 1945.

In 1945 he published *The Open Society and Its Enemies*. This was a two-volumed work, and opened with a spirited attack on **Plato**. Popper regarded Plato as an authoritarian thinker who is dogmatic and propagates a closed society. He also targeted **Hegel** as a dangerous absolutist, and **Marx**, who is condemned for his 'holism' and **determinism**. In Popper's view, Marx's propositions about **revolution** and the demise of **capitalism** cannot be scientific statements because they are presented as though they were unfalsifiable. Popper championed a reformist **liberalism** – a piecemeal engineering – and he considered economic planning by **states** as premised upon false certainty about society 'as a whole'

In 1946 Popper obtained the chair of logic and scientific method at the London School of Economics, and he occupied this post until his retirement in 1969. In 1957 he published his lively *Poverty of Historicism* where he argued that laws of history are necessarily bogus, since historical events are specific and unique. What are often presented as laws – by Marx, for example – are merely trends.

He received many distinctions and honours. He was a Fellow of the Royal Society, of the British Academy, and Membre de L'Institute de France.

In 1965 he was knighted and made a Companion of Honour in 1982.

See also: **Plato, Hegel, Marx, determinism, revolution, capitalism**

Further reading: Magee 1973

populism The term suggests a concern with the 'people'. It sometimes has elitist connotations and may be used pejoratively to suggest a cynical and manipulative 'politics' from on high.

Populism has been used to describe a number of different political movements. American agrarian movements were called populist because they championed the small farmer against city financiers whose policies were deemed inimical to the **interests** of the 'small man'. In Tsarist Russia, populism was a movement that idealised the peasantry and sought to base socialism around village communities. Some populists turned to a policy of assassination out of frustration and were fiercely criticised for this by **Lenin**.

In a positive use of the term, populism denotes a concern with ordinary people against the establishment and the **state**. It seeks to involve the masses in the political process, often bypassing representatives, and demanding the right to initiate legislation, vote in referenda, and the right of recall. It can be close to **anarchism** in its suspicion of conventional political processes and constitutes an important ingredient in **new social movements**.

In a pejorative sense the term denotes demagogic, often right-wing policies that appeal to the 'people' in a spirit of anti-liberalism. Here the 'people' are often those with a lower middle-class mentality – hostile to all who are different from the norm, gays, blacks, foreigners, and so on. In practice, populism of this kind has contempt for the mass of the population, but it is invoked as a way of discrediting intellectuals and those with expertise.

See also: **politics, Lenin, state, anarchism, new social movements**

Further reading: Canovan 1981

positivism Positivism is sometimes used to denote a 'scientific' approach, but positivism is far more than this.

It asserts that science can only deal with entities that

can be directly experienced. Positivism is based upon an empiricist rejection of value judgements and argues that science must be confined to the 'is' rather than the 'ought'. Positivism can be traced back to the **empiricism** of **Hume**, but in the nineteenth century it was developed by Comte (1798–1857) who sought to integrate all sciences into an overarching system of what he called 'positive philosophy'. Positivists have generally taken natural sciences as their 'model'.

Positivists seek to stress the quantitative aspects of political and social life, and **behaviouralism** is attracted to a positivist view of science.

The positivist view of society is now regarded as naïve. Imagine a discussion about **democracy** that does not indicate normative preferences. The attempt to separate facts from values denies that facts are relational, and it is out of the **relationships** that facts presuppose, that values emerge. The fact that **patriarchy** oppresses women and privileges men has obvious value implications, and attempts by positivist social scientists to devise a 'value-free' language have not been persuasive. Moreover, it is a myth that the natural sciences are value free, since debates over evolution, for example, have obvious implications for how we view the world. Even statements to do with the earth and the sun that are not controversial today proved tremendously contentious several hundred years ago!

The attempt to confine science to observable phenomena ends up, for all its objectivist pretensions, with a view of the world that limits the role of the scientist and social investigator.

See also: **Hume, behaviouralism, relationship, patriarchy**

Further reading: Guest 1996

postmodernism Closely linked to poststructuralism, post-modernism is an approach that developed in the 1970s and is a theory that spans art and literature, architecture and the social sciences. Because postmodernists empha-sise the importance of plurality and **difference**, they are sometimes unwilling to accept that they belong to an overarching 'school'. Nevertheless, it could be argued that they have the following features in common.

Postmodernists take the view that modernist and pre-modernist thought is characterised by what are called binary oppositions – sets of opposites in which one half is privileged and other downgraded – so that one has to make a choice between, for example, spirit and matter, men and women, truth and falsehood, and so on. Postmodernists argue that both 'partners' are relevant and one should not be privileged at the expense of the other.

Some postmodernists take the view that general the-ories should be avoided and that one should concentrate only upon the local and the particular. Others contend that because theories are expressions of **power**, these the-ories are all equally arbitrary or 'undecidable'. But it could be argued that such positions do not break with modernism, but express a scepticism or relativism that is as old as the hills. Postmodernism is a challenging theory but it is only helpful when it actually goes beyond modernity by linking theory and practice, and recon-structing the world as well as criticising it.

See also: **difference**
Further reading: Woods 1999

power A much-contested concept in political theory.

It is usually distinguished from **authority** on the grounds that whereas authority rests upon persuasion, power is exerted through intense social pressures that range from the manipulative to the coercive.

Power is conventionally seen as *negative* in character. Negative power is power 'over'. It involves a clear differentiation between the power-holder and the subordinate, whereas *positive* power is seen as power 'to'. Positive power 'empowers' others, and involves cooperation between the two parties.

Negative power is identified with **liberalism**. Positive power is a far older concept, but it has been rediscovered recently by contemporary writers who mistakenly believe that it is possible to have positive power without negative power. They seek to detach power from domination and **hierarchy**.

The problem with formulating power in 'purely' positive terms is that domination and **coercion** can come in through the back door, as it were. For example, **Arendt's** argument that even **slavery** involves organisation and **relationship** clearly does not mean that it does not *also* require the threat of **force** to sustain it. It is hard to see how the exercise of power in any form (however benign and developmental) can avoid the 'negative' attributes of hierarchy and an element of subordination. Power involves both the positive and the negative dimensions, since power is a form of **relationship** and it could be argued that it is impossible to conceptualise a relationship that does not involve a combination of power to and power over.

Power should be distinguished from force, since power requires compliance from a subject, whereas force involves treating another as a thing.

The debate that ensued in the 1960s and 1970s over the nature of power distinguished between power as decision-making (the most obvious manifestation of power), power as agenda-setting (important but less explicit) and power as the ability to shape people's consciousness, sometimes unintentionally and contingently.

This is the most difficult form of power to identify but it is clear that institutions like the media and the education system do exercise power, albeit as a by-product of their particular activities.

See also: **authority, liberalism, coercion, hierarchy, relationship, force**

Further reading: Haugaard 2002

praxis A term used to capture the unity of theory and practice, so that praxis is practice informed by theory.

Advocates often place themselves within the Marxist tradition, but advocate a version of **Marxism** that stresses the centrality of **Marx**'s *Economic and Philosophical Manuscripts* of 1844. They emphasise the importance of agency, and see **Engels** as a contaminating influence. They take particular issue with the theory of reflection – that truthful ideas reflect the reality of the external world more profoundly – and are sceptical about attempts to present Marxist ideas as a 'philosophy'. The idea that dialectical processes exist in the world of nature (as well as in society) is given short shrift, and they are strongly opposed to any reading of Marxism that is deterministic in character. The stress on will is, praxis theorists argue, central to Marx, and they identify the 'official' Marxism of the Communist Party **states** as a form of **positivism** – inimical to the humanistic and critical essence of Marx's own theory.

The work of **Gramsci** is often regarded as linked to the concept of praxis, and Gramsci referred to Marxism as a 'theory of praxis'. Praxis concepts have sometimes been important in the development of **Eurocommunism** and impacted upon some **New Left** versions of Marxism.

It is clear however that praxis theory developed at a time when it seemed obligatory for many intellectuals to state a formal adherence to Marx's theory, even though the division between Marx and Engels is problematic, and it could be argued that the attempt to distinguish radically between Marx's ideas and the propositions of **dialectical materialism** cannot be sustained. The positions of praxis theory are much closer to **anarchism** than to Marxist theory.

See also: **Marxism, Marx, Engels, Gramsci, Eurocommunism, New Left, dialectical materialism, anarchism**

Further reading: Hoffman 1975

property Property refers to the **rights** and duties that arise out of a relationship between a person and a thing. These 'things' may be physical but they need not be. Property rights can be abstract powers that a person or group have over their product, as in copyright, for example.

Property need not be exclusive. Property may belong to everyone, even if it is always regulated. Private property is contentious when it gives people **power** over others. Owning other persons as slaves is now seen as unacceptable, but the ownership of property that requires others to work for you is not. This latter situation, it could be argued, can mask real inequality as in the exchange process where money is given for services in a situation in which the two parties have very different amounts of real power.

Property is a social relationship, so that the ownership of things by individuals or groups can only be justified if it is conducive to development. This relates even to property in the person where a person's entitlement to own their bodies must depend upon rational usage. A person cannot be said to have unconditional ownership either of themselves or of objects in general, since all things are shaped by context, and this context imposes a **structure** upon them.

Thus, private property, like public property, is property that society considers it appropriate for individuals or particular groups to regulate in particular ways. Only a relational approach to property can divest it of the **abstraction** to which it is so prone.

See also: **relationship, power, structure, abstraction**
Further reading: Brace 2004

Proudhon, Pierre-Joseph (1809–65) Born in Besançon near the Swiss border. In 1827 he became a printer's apprentice.

He developed an extensive knowledge of Christian doctrine but this had the effect of making him an atheist and he identified God with tyranny and **property**. After winning a prize for an essay for the *Sunday Observance,* he wrote his *What is Property?* in which he espoused anarchy as 'the true form of **government**' and developed his famous paradox, 'Property is Theft'. His target was large-scale property and collectivism, and although he was prosecuted for his *Warning to Property Owners* that followed in 1842, he was acquitted on the grounds that the book was too complicated for ordinary people to understand!

He became interested in **dialectical** philosophy, went to Paris in 1844–5 where he clashed with **Marx** – whom he described as 'the tapeworm of socialism' – and published his two-volume *magnum opus System of Economic Contradictions* in 1846. He regarded communists as 'fanatics of **state power**'. He issued a manifesto in 1848, having been elected as a deputy to Parliament.

After Napoleon's *coup,* he was sent to prison for three years. Here he wrote *Confessions of a Revolutionary*, but his greatest work on ethics, *Justice in the Revolution and Church* (1858), brought him another three-year sentence. He fled to Belgium, and after his return urged abstention in the presidential elections of 1863.

Although he became increasingly conservative, espousing **nationalism, patriarchy** and anti-Semitism, he retained great influence over French workers, and his followers were the largest group to support the Paris Commune, six years after his death.

See also: **dialectics, Marx, nationalism, patriarchy**
Further reading: Woodcock 1956

public/private divide A concept that stresses the importance of separating what is public from what is private. The idea is alien to the ancient and medieval world where the notion of a society or individual autonomous from the **state** has yet to take root.

In its liberal form, the public/private divide sees the economy as a private mechanism that operates outside the state. It is increasingly recognised that industry not run by the state is nevertheless 'public' in character.

The distinction is a relative and fluid one, since what is private (when **conflict** is imperceptible) becomes public when society needs to intervene. Given concern with, for example, the spread of HIV/AIDS, and the advice given to people in the most intimate of their activities, it is difficult to see anything as inherently private in character.

Feminists have complained that the concept has been used to disadvantage women, by equating public activities with the conduct of men. Indeed, some feminists have even argued that the whole distinction should be overthrown. In fact, **feminism** insists that women have been oppressed through activities that have treated them as public beings when their privacy should be respected (for example, their marital status), so that it could be argued that the distinction should be retained. Rather it is a question of reformulating the public/private divide in an emancipatory manner.

The liberal tradition needs to be built upon, rather than

jettisoned. 'Publicising' private activities where the latter are not harmful is a denial of **freedom** so that the public/private divide is crucial to respect for personal liberty. Given the fact that the objective of the reformulation is to increase **equality**, it could be better characterised as a public/private difference, since the notion of a **division** implies a **conflict** that involves **force** and exclusion.

See also: **state, feminism, freedom, equality, division, conflict, force**

Further reading: Oliver 1999

R

radicalism A critical attitude that seeks to go to the root of things – to search out and challenge the principles that underpin institutions.

Radicalism is a disposition rather than a specific creed. Hence radicalism can be right wing as well as left wing. Although socialists have often been characterised as radical, in fact radical thought can seek to 'restore' society to, say, free **markets**. **Thatcher** can thus be considered a radical because she sought to break sharply with particular trends of social development, turning away from **state** expenditure on welfare.

Radical thought is often seen as doctrinaire, and radicals can indeed operate from abstract principles and disregard the complexities of reality. But radicalism need not be abstract, since it can be argued that going to the root of things is essential to a **realism** that is relevant and conscious of change.

Nor is it true that radicalism has to be revolutionary, in the sense of seeking to transform society through one concentrated political event. Reforms can be radical if they seek to establish a logic of transformation that leads from one change to another. Although **conservatism** is usually seen as the antithesis of radicalism, conservatives can become radical in situations in which they believe that root and branch transformation is necessary to establish a society they consider in keeping with their core values.

See also: **Thatcher**

Further reading: Arrighi et al. 1989

Rawls, John (1921–2002) Born in Baltimore, and after high school in Western Connecticut, he became a student at the University of Princeton in 1939.

He graduated in 1943 and saw military service in the Pacific, New Guinea and Japan. He continued postgraduate work at Princeton and spent a year at Oxford in 1952–3. From 1953 until 1959 he taught at Cornell University, but took a position at Harvard where he remained until his retirement.

In 1971 he published his most famous work, *A Theory of Justice*. Here he challenged the utilitarian view that laws ought to reflect the greatest happiness of the greatest number, fearing that this position could sacrifice the **interests** of the minority. He sought to develop a version of the **social contract** so that all would benefit. He made the traditional liberal freedoms a priority but argued that the distribution of basic social goods – income and wealth, self-respect – should also be equally distributed, unless an unequal distribution of the latter is to the advantage of the worst off.

In 1993 he published *Political Liberalism*. This acknowledged that in a free society, people inevitably have different views and values, but these can be reconciled if all accept a liberal conception based on what he called 'public reason'.

In 1999 he wrote *The Law of the Peoples* – a work that argues for an international norm of **justice** that allows other nations to intervene where people are persecuted by their **states**. Help should also be given to the impoverished.

He was awarded a number of prizes and held honorary degrees from Oxford and Harvard.

His *Collected Papers* were also published in 1999, and a revised edition of *A Theory of Justice* was brought out.

See also: **social contract, justice**

Further reading: Woolf 1977

realism A concept that is used in a variety of ways in political theory.

Sometimes the word is used in place of materialism. A realist is someone who accepts that the world is external to our ideas, and we can measure the truth of our ideas as reflections of, or **reconstructions** of, this external reality.

Realism can also denote a current in international-relations theorising that accepts the **state** as a given. Realists in this context may even argue that international relations should be separated from **politics**, since politics, they argue, is about the state, whereas international relations deals with exchanges between states in a world in which there is no global state to regulate affairs. This approach has been partially discredited by those who see international institutions, whether transnational corporations or agents like the United Nations, as having significant implications for order and the ability of people to govern their own lives. Critics of realism question the equation of politics with the state.

Realism poses a challenge. Is reality simply the world as it is, or should we see reality as the world as it is *becoming*? The danger with those who consider themselves realists is that they cling to a snapshot view of 'reality' that ignores the change that is occurring. Hence a static conception of realism can distort reality. On the other hand, anti-realists are vulnerable to the charge that their 'ideals' do not relate meaningfully to the external world.

It could be argued that realism needs to be woven into **utopianism** so that the world is seen as a process of transformation, and alternatives are promoted that are rooted in the real world.

See also: **state, politics, utopianism**
Further reading: Berki 1981

reconstruction   More than a critique: to reconstruct a concept is to rework it in the light of new circumstances.

It is impossible to reconstruct a concept without deconstructing it, that is, criticising it from within. Terms need to be criticised for their abstractness and exclusiveness, but this criticism is not enough.

To reconstruct a concept is to build something new out of the something old, so that we move beyond the past and look to the future. It might be argued that not all concepts can be reconstructed. Only those that are **momentum concepts** can be reconstructed, for they have a logic that is progressive and emancipatory in character. Static concepts cannot be reconstructed, for they are divisive and imply repression and exclusion. Thus concepts like **patriarchy**, violence and the **state** cannot be reconstructed as they are incompatible with an emancipated world.

Reconstruction cannot be taken to mean that a concept is reworked in a way that makes it final, wholly transparent, absolutely true. Reconstruction takes concepts like **equality** and **freedom** and gives them a more inclusive content, but it must be stated that this reworking reflects new circumstances that will themselves become old and one-sided. Reconstruction is thus a process that continues into the future, and although reconstructed concepts are more truthful than archaic ones, they cannot be said to be the last word on the subject.

See also: **momentum concept, emancipation, equality, freedom, patriarchy, state**

Further reading: Peterson 1992

relationship A concept that emphasises the importance of linkage. It breaks with the liberal idea that individuals should be conceived of as self-contained atoms.

Individuals can only identify themselves in relationship with others, so that it is misleading to picture the individual opposed to society if by this is meant that individuals are not themselves social in character.

Because relationships are multiple and distinctive, each individual is unique as the embodiment of an infinite set of relationships. Although relationships are necessarily hierarchical, they are emancipatory if they are fluid and egalitarian, and people can 'change places'. Relationships only become oppressive when they are fixed, unilateral and justify domination through stereotyping the relatively passive agent or party.

See also: **emancipation**

Further reading: Hoffman 1998

representation A concept that involves making present, or re-presenting, individuals or groups who are themselves absent. Representatives act on behalf those whom they represent.

Under **liberalism** the idea extends to all individuals, in theory at any rate, who regard the ruler as their representative, and therefore the ruler is themselves writ large.

Writers like **Rousseau** are hostile to representation on the grounds that the power to make laws can never be alienated from the citizen. Others like **Burke** take the view that representatives can act autonomously from those they represent, judging issues quite independently.

Both views are one-sided. All **relationships** are representational, in that the person who takes a **leadership** role on a particular issue can be said to be representing the other. Historically, the notion that **government** could and should be representative broke with the old view that only direct control counts. In practice, government is a mixture of the direct and indirect, since it is impossible to organise without some degree of concentration, and the formation of committees, for example, constitutes a necessary form of representation.

Should representatives be identical to those whom they represent? This is a mechanical notion that assumes that sameness and **difference** can be radically spliced apart. Representatives should clearly have something in common with those whom they represent, but they are also different, often in the education they have and the confidence they possess. What representatives need is empathy – a capacity to understand those they represent – so that one would expect black people or women, for example, to understand the problems that other blacks and women experience better than male or white representatives do. On the other hand, groups are far from homogenous, so that it is important not to assume that representatives have to be identical to those they represent.

See also: **liberalism, Rousseau, relationship, government, difference**

Further reading: Birch 1971

republicanism A particular approach to the **state**, republicanism rejects traditional monarchy where the king or queen has the realm as a personal possession and regards the ruled as subjects.

Although republicanism has its origins in the city-states in ancient Greece, it came to be seen as synonymous with 'virtue' in ancient Rome, with republican rule denoting a regime in which citizens conducted their common affairs for the common good. Luxury and corruption are enemies to republican **freedom**, and republicanism emphasises participation in rule, a belief in 'balance' between monarchical, aristocratic and 'democratic' elements.

The public good must prevail over the private pursuit of wealth, the common good over factionalism. Republicanism does not necessarily oppose monarchy within a 'mixed' constitution, and in the late eighteenth century, republicanism became tied to the idea of **representation**. It was possible therefore for republics to be large states, with diverse populations, and with considerable emphasis still upon virtue.

Utilitarians defended republicanism as an effective and economical way of conducting the affairs of the state, but republicanism is sometimes contrasted with **liberalism**. The argument is that whereas liberalism stresses private **interests** and emphasises the importance of the **market** and the pursuit of private profit, republicanism stresses devotion to the **community** and the common good. Whereas liberalism may be tempted to define freedom in negative and individualistic terms, republicans see freedom as positive and social in character. Participation is the hallmark of the citizen: apathy and passivity are the negation of **citizenship** responsibility.

See also: **state, freedom, representation, liberalism, market, citizenship**

Further reading: Petit 1997

revolution The term generally denotes a transformation from one form of the **state** to another, and is usually held to involve violence.

However, revolutions need not be violent. Revolution can be constitutional and peaceful under certain circumstances.

The term denotes some kind of progress. Although revolutions sometimes refer to any radical change in state form, it could be argued that this ignores the distinction between revolution and counter-revolution, the latter being a change of state form that moves backwards, **fascism** being a good example.

Revolution involves transforming society itself, since any meaningful change of state requires a different kind of society underpinning it. The change in state form is the culmination of a process that is rooted in social change. This helps us to differentiate revolution from a mere *coup d'état*, the latter having an elitist connotation that suggests superficial change.

Revolution can only succeed in societies in which liberal freedoms are denied. Where liberal freedoms have been acquired, then attempts to secure revolution of a traditional type can only fizzle out into **terrorism** or at best a *coup*.

A broader use of the term revolution can be employed to denote not a single and dramatic event (like the French or Russian revolutions) but a process of radical change. This use of the term dissolves the contrast between revolution and reform, since where the latter is meaningful, it requires a revolution in social mores and technology. Here revolution points to critique, and is relevant to all societies since the only constant in life is change itself.

See also: **state, fascism**
Further reading: Skocpol 1979

rights The demand for rights usually suggests that the existing law is deficient and should be altered.

Although historically rights might be enjoyed differentially by particular groups in society, the great advance of the liberal tradition is the assertion that all have rights.

The problem, however, is that rights need to be linked to resources. The right to dine at the Ritz, for example, does not mean very much to someone without the resources to do so. The assertion of rights should be seen, therefore, as a challenge, so that when they are won, rights need to be critically evaluated as to how they transform peoples' lives.

Right is a good example of a **momentum concept** since rights are continually expanding and changing. We are aware now, for example, of the right to a smoke-free environment in a way we were not even a few years ago. We can be sure that the rights we now claim will be built upon and expanded in the future.

Rights need to be analysed concretely so that account is taken of context. The rights that citizens enjoy in an emergency will obviously differ from those to which we are entitled in 'normal' times. Rights also differ according to an infinite number of **differences** – the rights of the elderly and of children obviously differ from those enjoyed by young and healthy men and women.

Rights necessarily generate responsibilities. Rights involve duties and it is impossible to have one without the other. Hence rights belong to humans, rather than to foetuses, animals, and so on. Nor is it possible for an individual to enjoy a right at another's expense. Hence we need to be able to distinguish between rights and privileges. Rights develop people; privileges generate insecurity and divide society.

See also: **momentum concept, difference**
Further reading: Waldron 1984

Rothbard, Murray (1926–95) Educated in New York City and studied at Columbia University. His doctoral thesis (1956) was on welfare economics.

In 1965 he edited *Left and Right* (through to 1968), and published a biography on the Austrian free marketeer Ludwig von Mises. He was particularly interested in the problem of economic depression, and in 1970 he wrote a book exposing what he called 'The Hoover Myth'. He produced a Libertarian Manifesto, entitled *For a New Liberty*, that was published in 1973. He also wrote on the American colonies in the seventeenth century (1975) and the first half of the eighteenth century (1976) and complained of **Nozick's** 'immaculate conception of the **state**'. He edited the *Journal of Libertarian Studies* through to 1995, and published a major work in 1982, *The Ethics of Liberty*. He was made a Distinguished Professor of Economics, at the University of Nevada, Las Vegas, describing **Marx** in 1990 as a religious eschatologist.

In all, he wrote twenty-five books and thousands of articles and Volumes One and Two of his history of economic thought appeared just after his death.

He was devoutly anti-socialist as well as being anti-statist, and in 1993 he declared that 'in an age of galloping statism, the classical liberal, the advocate of the free **market**, has an obligation to carry the struggle to all levels of society'.

He had been bitterly opposed to Roosevelt's New Deal. He identified with the Confederates, the anti-federalists and objected to taxation. Indeed, he argued that the taxing power defines the state in the same way that theft defines a robber. The only civil **rights** are **property** rights.

See also: **Nozick, Marx, state, rights**
Further reading: Raimondo 2000

Rousseau, Jean-Jacques (1712–78) Born in Geneva. At the age of 16 went to Chambery in France.

In 1749 he wrote *Discourse on the Sciences and Arts* and a year later he further expanded his reputation with a *Discourse on the Origins of Inequality* – a work that saw humans as living peacefully in a 'state of nature' until corrupted by the state and technology.

In 1758 he wrote *Letters to d'Alembert,* and in 1762 he published *Emile* in which he made the case for a **'natural'** education. The work contained an explicit defence of male domination and has been an understandable target of much feminist criticism.

Far and away his most significant political work was *The Social Contract* in which he sought to establish a form of the state that would be **legitimate**, so that people obeyed laws they had prescribed to themselves. He championed the idea of the general will – a controversial notion that argued that the particular will of individuals must harmonise with the overall will of the **community**. Rousseau excluded women, unbelievers and the poor from the body of lawmaking citizens. He was opposed to **representation**, believing that **sovereignty** itself could never be delegated.

The French parliament ordered that *The Social Contract* be burned, and Rousseau fled to Neuchâtel, then under the control of Prussia. In 1761 he wrote *Letters from a Mountain* in which he defended freedom of religion. This provoked further attacks, and he went to Britain before returning to France in 1767.

In 1770 he finished his *Confessions*, a remarkable autobiographical account that was followed by two further autobiographical writings, *Dialogues* (between 1772 and 1776) and *Reveries of the Solitary Walker,* written between 1776 and 1778.

See also: **state, natural, feminism, legitimacy, representation, sovereignty**
Further reading: Shklar 1969

S

Saint-Simon, Claude-Henri (1760–1825) The son of a minor
noble, Saint-Simon was born in Paris. A supporter of the
French **Revolution** in 1789, he immediately renounced
his title, but was imprisoned during the Terror. He was
released after spending nine months in captivity, and
became convinced that a programme of social reorganisation was needed.

His first book on political theory, *Letters of a Genevan
to his Contemporaries*, was published in 1802. This was
followed by *Introduction to the Work of Science in the
19th Century* (1807), *Memoir on the Science of Man*
(1813), *On the Reorganisation of European Society*
(1814), and *The New Christianity* (1825). In this final
work he argued that a new religion led by the most able
thinkers in society (scientists and artists) would express
dominant beliefs for a new industrial order.

Saint-Simon argued that Europe was in 'critical
disequilibrium' and would soon undergo reconstruction.
He argued strongly for a planned economy. He suggested
a framework of three chambers: one body made up of
engineers and artists to propose plans; a second of scientists responsible for assessing the plans; and a third group
of industrialists whose task would be that of implementing the schemes according to the **interests** of the whole
community.

After his death in 1825, a group of his followers published *An Explanation of the Doctrine of Saint-Simon*.
They interpreted Saint-Simon as a socialist and argued for

the redistribution of wealth for the benefit of society. Saint-Simon's theories also influenced figures such as Herzen, Carlyle and J. S. Mill. Engels is said to have taken the notion of the withering away of the state from Saint-Simon.

See also: community, Mill, Engels, state

Further reading: Ionescu 1976

Sartre, Jean-Paul (1905–80) Born in Paris. He graduated from the Ecole Normale Supérieure in 1929. During the war, he was first imprisoned and then joined the resistance movement. In 1939 he published *La Nausée*.

In 1943 he published his major work *Being and Nothingness*. Here he argues that people are the totality, not only of what they are, but also of what they do not yet have, and what they might have been. Others are limitation on one's **freedom**, a 'hell', so that Sartre is basically pessimistic about the capacity of people to cooperate and secure **emancipation**.

After the war, he wrote a number of plays including *Huis Clos* (1945) and *Le Diable et le Bon Dieu* (1952). A work on literature (1947) links art to the pursuit of freedom. Though not actually a member of the French Communist Party, Sartre was concerned to reconcile existentialism and **Marxism**. In 1960 he wrote *The Critique of Dialectical Reason* where he seeks to distinguish between humans who are simply in a 'series' – for example, queuing to catch a bus – and a 'group in fusion', where like-minded people participate in revolutionary **politics** to change the world.

In 1956 Sartre spoke out angrily against the crushing of the Hungarian uprising, and he denounced the intervention in Czechoslovakia in 1968. He was targeted by the right-wing terrorist group resisting Algerian independence, and in 1967 he was involved with Bertrand Russell's International War Crimes

Tribunal set up to judge the activity of the USA in Vietnam. He supported the student rebellion in Paris the following year.

His biography on the novelist Flaubert was a massive undertaking, and he produced four volumes between 1960 and 1971, using Freudian and Marxian analyses. *L'Idiot* was never finished.

See also: **freedom, emancipation, Marxism**
Further reading: Aronson 1980

Schmitt, Carl (1888–1985) Born into a Catholic family in Westphalia.

A conservative critic of the Weimar republic, his career was tainted by the fact that he joined the Nazi Party and became director of the University Teachers' Group of the National Socialist League. He wrote his major work (translated into English in 1976) in 1927 – *The Concept of the Political*. Here he argues that the friend/enemy distinction is a necessary feature of all political communities. Indeed what defines the 'political' as opposed to other human activities is the intensity of feeling toward friends and enemies, or toward one's own and those perceived as hostile outsiders.

His hostility to liberal **democracy** has attracted some contemporary theorists to his work.

See also: **politics, democracy**
Further reading: Bendersky 1983

slavery Not just an institution but a concept as well. Slavery involves the domination of one person or group by another, and slaves lack some or all the **rights** that those who dominate them enjoy.

The ancient world took it for granted that civilization was only possible on the basis of slavery. Here slavery was seen in *chattel* terms, making it possible for some to own the persons of others. Chattel slavery continues in the medieval period, and even liberals like **Locke** could endorse this kind of slavery, arguing that slaves were war criminals whose lives had been pardoned.

Indeed it is worth noting that **liberalism** with its doctrine of private **property** only rejects slavery towards the end of the eighteenth century, and it is revealing that **Rousseau**, while challenging the notion of slavery as **natural**, can still suggest that slavery and **citizenship** may go together.

The term comes to mean the absence of some rights rather than all rights. The reference by **Marx** to wage slaves points to workers who may have political and legal rights, but are still subject to the despotism of capital. Feminists see women as slaves, particularly in periods when they have no social, political and legal identity of their own, and the term implies someone who is not emancipated, someone who is unable to govern their own life.

Slavery in all its forms is a **relationship**, and therefore although **force** and the threat of force exists in the background, slaves must, albeit in a nominal sense, 'agree' to their servitude. This relational position is also important because it stresses the mutuality of the degradation that slavery involves: masters are enslaved to their slaves, since they too lack meaningful **freedom**.

See also: **rights, Locke, liberalism, property, natural, Rousseau, citizenship, Marx, feminism, relationship, force, freedom**

Further reading: Finley 1980

Smith, Adam (1723–90) Born in Kirkcaldy in Fife, and studied at Glasgow University. In 1751 he was appointed professor of logic at this university and two years later he took the chair of moral philosophy.

In 1759 he published his *Theory of Moral Sentiments* in which he argued that sympathy lies at the heart of our moral norms. Habits are socially acquired, and they vary according to time and place, depending upon whether the means of subsistence is based on hunting, animal husbandry, agriculture or commerce.

In 1763, Smith obtained a position as tutor to the young Duke of Buccleuch. He was able to visit France, and meet economists and philosophes. His *Inquiry into the Nature and Causes of the Wealth of Nations* appeared in 1776. The work polemicised against mercantilism, and argued passionately for free trade. Under conditions of competition, the pursuit of self-interest leads to the good of society as a whole. Markets expand, capital accumulates and productivity increases as a result of the division of labour.

But although Smith is seen as the founder of modern economics, he saw moral philosophy as an integral part of political economy. He raised critical questions about **capitalism**, and showed that from a moral point of view, the effect of the **market** on the human personality could be problematic. He followed his good friend **Hume** in arguing that the **state** arose not as the product of a **social contract**, but through habitual deference to **authority**. He championed the rule of law, and saw that the state had a limited but important role not only in providing security but also in sponsoring both education to overcome the effects of the division of labour and public works where there were market failures.

In 1778 he was appointed Commissioner of Customs in Edinburgh.

See also: **capitalism, market, state, social contract, authority**

Further reading: Raphael 1985

social contract This concept points to the formation of the state as a result of contract between individuals. The idea arose as part of the classical liberal tradition, and is tied to a belief that individuals exist separately in a state of nature before coming together to form a state.

The great strength of the idea is that individuals can and must act rationally as equals, since the notion of contract provides a sense of exchange. Individuals need to **consent** to **government** and authorise acts that are made in their name.

The problem with the concept is that it is presented abstractly. Individuals are seen as separate and isolated entities so that the formation of a society is presented as a deliberate creation. In fact, people acquire their identity as individuals through their **relationships** with others, so that the idea that society is 'created' by individuals is insupportable. Moreover, the notion of rationality is seen as a static attribute rather than something that develops as a result of education, resources and practice.

Not only is the idea of a society based on contract wholly fanciful, but the notion that the state with its acts of **force** can be authorised, is also (it could be argued) equally implausible. Although states from time to time speak of a 'social contract' with their populations, the notion is abstract and misleading, and should be seen as inherent in the problematic character of liberalism in general, and classical **liberalism** in particular.

See also: **state, consent, government, relationship, force**
Further reading: Barker 1946

Sorel, Georges (1847–1922) Born in Cherbourg. He attended the Ecole Polytechnique, and entered the civil service as an engineer.

He published nothing before he was 39. In *Le Procès de Socrate* (1889) and *La Ruin du Monde Antique* (1894,

1901) he argued that a strong moral **structure** rested upon a sturdy family; a warrior mentality; and an 'epic state of mind' rooted in myth. He became a socialist in 1892, arguing that workers overcome their own 'natural natures' through acting heroically.

In 1906 he wrote the *Social Foundations of Contemporary Economics* where, although he praised **Marx**, he was particularly hostile to the idea that violent **conflict** would come to an end in a higher communist society.

In 1908 he wrote *The Illusions of Progress*. Here he argued that the notion of **dialectical** progress in Marx's writings would sap the vitality of workers' organisations and subject them to an aristocracy of **state** functionaries. He became a **syndicalist**, taking the view that workers' organisations ought to act through strikes and direct action rather than through conventional political involvement. Myths, he argued, were ideas that steeled people with certainty and moral purpose, and he famously spoke of the 'myth' of the general strike. This was an idea that would mobilise workers into action.

He elaborates this point in his *Reflections on Violence* (1908). Here he speaks of the 'social poetry' that sustains moral energy. After 1908 he became pessimistic about the future of the workers' movement, and until 1914 he thought that royalism could provide the moral inspiration needed for action. He showed some sympathy for **fascism**, especially in Mussolini's Italy. In his final years he welcomed the Russian **Revolution** in the hope that it would bring about self-governing workers' councils.

See also: **Marx, conflict, state, syndicalism, fascism**
Further reading: Stanley 1981

sovereignty A concept that denotes absolute **power**. It is normally associated with the unlimited power of the **state**, so that some argue that states can only be identified through their sovereignty.

Although there is an argument that sovereignty as a statist concept only emerges with the modern state, the very character of the state as an institution claiming a monopoly of legitimate **force** suggests a claim to sovereignty. But what is this state sovereignty? One influential international-relations writer sees sovereignty as a constitutional and legal independence that does not depend upon external recognition, and hence argues that Rhodesia (that declared its unilateral independence under Ian Smith in 1965) was a sovereign state. This seems very problematic, and sovereignty is usually identified with the capacity of the state to effectively impose its will on society at large.

But this returns us to the problem of the state. Since the state can only claim a monopoly of **legitimate** force because there are those who resist this claim, so state sovereignty is subject to the same problem. This sovereignty is only declared because it is challenged, and the more flamboyantly it is declared, the more obviously it is resisted.

Sovereignty is better defined in terms of individuals rather than states – the sovereign individual being the person who can govern their own life. It is important to see this as a concept towards which we need to move, but can never actually reach. Moreover, we should not think of individuals as isolated atoms, but as people who relate to one another, so that the sovereignty of one person is influenced by the sovereignty of all.

See also: **state, legitimacy**
Further reading: Hoffman 1998

Stalin, Joseph (1879–1953) Born in Georgia. Educated in the Tiflis Theological Seminary.

In 1901 he joined the Social Democratic Labour Party, and siding with the Bolsheviks he became editor of *Pravda*. He supported the Russian **Revolution** and was appointed Commissar of Nationalities.

He played an important part in winning the civil war, supported **Lenin**'s New Economic Policy – to allow small-scale free enterprise to operate – and in April 1922 became general secretary of the party. He removed the supporters of **Trotsky**, and Lenin's attempt to have Stalin removed from his office did not succeed.

In 1928 he reversed the New Economic Policy (initiated by Lenin), and thousands of richer peasants were executed. Trotsky was pushed out of **government**, and banished to Kazakhstan. The first Five Year Plan was introduced in 1928 and there were massive increases in coal, iron and electricity.

Following the assassination of one of Stalin's critics, Kirov, Stalin had old Bolsheviks who disagreed with his policy arrested and executed. The Red Army was purged, and many of its officers shot, and the secret police, the NKVD, was also purged.

Convinced that Britain was in favour of a Nazi thrust eastwards, he signed the Nazi–Soviet pact in 1939. Stalin refused to believe that Germany would invade in 1941, and although the Germans were initially very successful, they were defeated at Stalingrad. A second front was opened up by Britain and the USA. Following the dropping of the atomic bomb by the USA, lease aid to the devastated USSR was stopped. Relations with the former allies deteriorated, and the cold war began. The West succeeded in maintaining their presence in West Berlin.

A further purge of the party was contemplated when Stalin died.

Stalin gained much of his support as a populariser whose expositions of Marxist philosophy were clear and concise.

See also: **Lenin, Trotsky**
Further reading: Deutscher 1966

state The state is an institution that claims to be sovereign over a particular society. Theorists differ as to whether the state primarily uses **force** to order society or relies essentially upon **morality**.

Some argue that the state is based upon **force**. In **Weber's** classic definition, the state is an institution that claims a monopoly of **legitimate** force for a particular territory. It is clear that while force is central to identifying the state, this force has to be monopolised, legitimate and focussed territorially.

Others link the state to morality, arguing that the state is rooted in our notion of what is right. These writers do not deny that states use force: they merely argue that this is not its central attribute.

Others argue that the state is so complex that it is impossible to define. **Easton,** for example, contends that it would be better to speak of a political system rather than a state.

There is not only disagreement about what the state is, but also about when it arose. Those who identify the state with morality tend to argue that only the modern (or liberal) state should be called a state, since earlier polities were unable to sharply divide what is public from the private, control the lives of all in society, and make a distinction between an office and the individual holding it.

Whereas the 'morality' school shows little interest in states' origins (although **Rousseau** is an exception here) or argues (as in the case of **Green**) that states have always existed, the 'force' school raises the question as to why states emerge, and what made it possible for early tribal societies (like contemporary international society) to resolve **conflicts** through using sanctions of a non-statist kind. This makes it possible to at least ask as to whether it would be possible domestically for people to govern themselves without the state.

See also: **morality, force, legitimacy, Weber, Easton, Rousseau, Green**

Further reading: Dunleavy and O'Leary 1987

Stirner, Max (1806–56) Born Johann Kaspar Schmidt at Bayreuth in Bavaria. He studied at the University of Berlin from 1826 to 1928 where he attended the lectures of **Hegel**.

He returned to Berlin in 1832 and managed to get a teacher's certificate. But the Prussian **government** refused to appoint him to a full-time post. He married in 1837 but his wife died in childbirth a few months later. He acquired a post at a girls' school and was able to associate with **Young Hegelians** like the Bauer brothers.

He wrote an article 'the False Principle of our Education' for **Marx's** *Rheinische Zeitung* (Rhineland Gazette) in 1842, and in 1845 published his principal work, *The Ego and His Own*.

Influenced by Hegelianism, he saw history as culminating in the sovereign individual, which is unique and creates everything. Because he argued that sovereign individuals must emancipate themselves from society, he was dubbed 'Saint Max' by **Marx** and **Engels** in the ferocious critique they wrote of him (and other left Hegelians) in *The German Ideology*.

He married a member of the Young Hegelian circle, and although he had adopted the *nom de plume* Max Stirner so as not to alarm the head of the school where he taught, he lost his job. He spent the rest of his life in poverty.

To earn a living, he translated the work of English

economists. In 1852, four years before his death, he wrote a *History of Reaction.*

See also: **Hegel, Young Hegelians, Marx, Engels**

Further reading: McLellan 1969

structure A concept that denotes linkages that occur independent of intention and aim.

Structures are crucial to scientific study, since without identifying a structure, no explanation is possible. Structures occur in nature as well as in society, and social structures denote patterns that occur independently of the human will. By this is meant that humans organise their lives in ways that they do not intend: there is necessarily a difference between what we think we are doing, and what actually happens in practice. In class-divided societies, people are capitalists or workers, for example.

Human society will always be structural. Whether they like it or not, people are men or women, black or white, northerners or southerners, and so on. The presence of structures in society does not negate the existence of **agency**. Structures are the product of our activity, but the point is that we only grasp them imperfectly and one-sidedly. The idea put forward by some structuralists, that the text as structure cannot have an author, wrongly assumes that (social) structures are not themselves the product of human activity.

It does not follow that because structures are universal, they are timeless in character. On the contrary, structures change – according to an evolutionary time-scale in the world of nature – and through history in society.

Structuralists who posit the existence of language as a system that structures reality take a one-sided view of the language we speak. Language alters society, but the way that words change the world have results that always differ from the intentions we have.

The problem with many post-structuralists is that they reject the one-sidedness of 'structuralism' only to substitute a one-sidedness of their own. Once structures are seen as the product of, and always subject to, change, then the argument that these structures do not exist independently of our consciousness becomes redundant.

See also: **agency**

Further reading: Pettit 1975

syndicalism Closely linked to **anarchism**, and sometimes called 'anarcho-syndicalism', syndicalism stresses the importance of trade unions in the struggle for an emancipated society.

The trade unions can only be vehicles for syndicalism if they are aloof from the limited objectives of 'bread and butter' issues (the traditional fare of trade unionism), and are not entangled with conventional politicians and the policies of the **state**. It espouses strikes and direct action by the workers, and thus is opposed to, and opposed by, Marxist political parties.

Syndicalists stress the importance of local action against centralised bodies and tend to be powerful where liberal traditions are weak and conventional **politics** has been discredited.

The Confederación Nacional dey Trabajo in Spain had massive support from workers who were hostile to the state and organised religion, and it played an important role during the Spanish civil war, clashing with the communists, social democrats and liberal republicans. The American International Workers of the World or Wobblies were significant before and during the First World War, but drew heavily upon support from immigrant workers.

Syndicalism is often violent in its tactics, and its association with theorists like **Sorel** has often led its critics to argue that it has an ideologically ambiguous character.

See also: **anarchism, state, Marxism, politics**
Further reading: Cole 1973

T

terrorism Generally regarded as the use of violence to obtain political ends. This concept has been much debated recently as a result of a rise in terrorism throughout the world.

The term is usually used pejoratively, although some fundamentalists are willing to identify their movements positively as being terrorist in character. The problem is that because terrorism is such a grisly phenomenon, it is usually condemned rather than thoughtfully analysed, and it is even argued that to try to understand terrorism is somehow to condone it.

The term is rather loosely used to describe all forms of political violence, but it could be argued that the term terrorism ought to be reserved for those acts of violence that are perpetrated when non-violent forms of protest and political activity are disallowed. In other words, terrorism arises when people cannot meaningfully protest in non-violent ways.

In anti-liberal societies, like apartheid South Africa, for example, the resort to violence by the African National Congress cannot be described as terrorism, since no other form of protest was permissible, even though as a result of this violence, harm resulted not simply to **property** and **state** functionaries, but also to innocent bystanders. Political violence becomes terrorism only in societies where liberal freedoms prevail, and where, it has to be said, the use of **force** by protesters is almost certain to be counter-productive as it would alienate most of the public.

States must bear some of the responsibility for terrorism, since the state itself by using violence to tackle conflicts of interest, normalises the use of force, and inverts the arguments of terrorism rather than overcomes them. It is important that terrorism be placed in the wider context of violence itself, since its use arises where inequalities and chauvinistic policies prevent people from 'changing places'. While the eradication of terrorism is difficult, it is not impossible. But what is required are imaginative policies and a movement towards a world in which people can settle their differences through negotiation and compromise.

See also: **property, state, force**

Further reading: Laqueur 2003

Thatcher, Margaret (1925–) Born in Grantham. She read chemistry at Oxford, and in 1959 was elected Member of Parliament for Finchley. Within just two years she had been appointed parliamentary secretary at the Ministry of Pensions, and in 1970 she became Secretary of State for Education.

In February 1975 (after Heath had lost the election in 1974), she was elected leader of the Conservative Party, becoming Britain's first female prime minister in May 1979. In April 1982, she dispatched a Royal Navy task force in a war with Argentina: a year later the Conservatives won the largest landslide election victory since 1945. The Irish Republican Army let off a bomb in Brighton in 1984 in retaliation for the death of the hunger strikers four years earlier.

Income tax was cut, and alongside privatisation, restrictions were placed on trade union activity. 1984 saw the beginning of the year-long miners' strike.

During her third term in office she brought in the 'community charge' or the 'poll tax' that proved deeply unpopular.

The **government** was also divided over the European Union, with Thatcher rejecting any form of integration with Europe. In November 1990, Geoffrey Howe resigned, and following a leadership ballot, she resigned. In 1992 she took a seat in the House of Lords. The following year, she published *The Downing Street Years* followed by *The Path to Power.* She backed Hague and then Iain Duncan Smith as Party leaders, and her intervention in 1999 in the Pinochet extradition case attracted considerable media coverage.

Thatcher is best known for her passionate belief in free **markets** and her hostility to the provision of public welfare. She saw the welfare state as a kind of **state** socialism, sapping the independence of the individual and forcing people to pay large amounts of tax.

Following a series of minor strokes in late 2001, she was advised by her doctors to retire from public life. In March 2002 she published *Statecraft: Strategies for a Changing World.*

Further reading: Young 1991

third way The third way is a concept that seeks a political path between liberal **capitalism** and traditional socialism.

The concept has been employed both by the right and the left. The right used the notion particularly in the 1930s to present a programme that was neither capitalist nor communist in character.

Some communists who were critical of the Communist Party **states** saw in the third way a strategy that would avoid both **liberalism** and Stalinism, but it has recently been formulated to indicate a strategy that rejects both **conservatism** and what is seen as 'old-fashioned' socialism.

Critics of the concept argue that the notion is simply a gimmick that fails to accept the need to recognise the basic character of a class-divided society.

See also: **Giddens**

Further reading: Giddens 1998

Tocqueville, Alexis de (1805–59) Born into a royalist aristocratic family, his father having narrowly escaped execution from the **Jacobins**. Tocqueville entered **government** service in 1827 but found it impossible to support the new Orleanist monarchy established in the July **Revolution** of 1830.

Between 1831 and 1832 he visited the USA, and his *Democracy in America* appeared in two parts – in 1835 and 1840. The book won him international acclaim and after the second part appeared, he was elected to the Académie française. In the book he argued that **democracy** requires religion and individualistic customs, and he was struck by the high levels of local participation in the American polity. Yet it could be argued that the book is really about American **liberalism** rather than democracy.

In 1835 he visited Ireland, and noted the growing rift between Catholics and Protestants. In 1839 he was elected deputy in Normandy and remained a member of the Chamber until 1848. After the February Revolution of 1848 he was elected to the Constituent Assembly and served on the commission that drew up the republican constitution. He was elected to the new Legislative Assembly in 1849, and for a few months was minister for foreign affairs. He was bitterly opposed to Louis Napoleon's coup d'état, an event that ended Tocqueville's political career.

In 1856 he published his unfinished masterpiece *The Ancient Regime* in which he characterised the French

Revolution as the greatest **property** transaction in history. He also corresponded with J. S. **Mill.**

See also: **Jacobins, liberalism, democracy, property, Mill**

Further reading: Lively 1962

toleration A concept that denotes an acceptance of differing activities and thought.

Toleration implies a deliberate act, since one cannot be said to tolerate activity or ideas of which one is unaware or to which one is indifferent. Toleration relates to ideas or conduct of which one disapproves, so it would be wrong to ascribe toleration to accepting something with which one agrees.

As an ideal, toleration arises with **liberalism,** where it is initially applied to certain kinds of religious observance. The idea becomes more inclusive as it extends not only to all religious activity, but also to ideas and conduct in general.

Toleration should be extended to all ideas and activities that do not harm. To tolerate intolerant ideas is one thing, but it is impossible to tolerate conduct that does not tolerate your own activity. Of course, it is possible and even desirable to challenge ideas and actions of which one disapproves. This is compatible with toleration provided that the person challenged is being persuaded rather than coerced. Rational argument accords with toleration; suppression does not.

In general, a tolerant person or society errs on the side of leniency. It is important that the question of harm is rigorously justified, and since the suppression of a harmful activity is costly and dangerous, it should only be applied when rational argument has failed to make a dent in activity that prevents others from carrying out their **legitimate** activities.

In other words, although intolerance may be necessary, it should be carried out in the interests of toleration itself.
See also: **liberalism, legitimacy**
Further reading: Horton and Mendus 1999

Tolstoy, Leo (1828–1910) Born in Tula province, Russia. In 1844 he went Kazan University. In 1851 he joined an artillery regiment and was greatly influenced by Cossack peasants.

His first novel was entitled *Childhood*. He left the army in 1856 and wrote about the appalling experiences he had in the Crimean war. Witnessing a public guillotining in France, he became a life-long opponent of the **state**. The school that he established for peasant children on the family estate saw education as a freely adopted activity. The school was later raided by police.

Between 1863 and 1869 he wrote his celebrated novel *War and Peace*, emphasising the role of chance and circumstance in the moulding of great events. In *Anna Karenina* (1874–82) he explores the tension between vitality and pointlessness, and his *Confession* of 1882 showed his growing interest in religion. In demoting the role of 'great men', Tolstoy declared war on corruption, ostentation and inequality.

He saw in the Gospels a creed of cosmopolitan **equality**. He regarded patriotism as anathema, and argued that persuasion, not **force**, should be used against evil. He became a vegetarian, and sought to alleviate famine victims. In *The Kingdom of God is Within You* (1894) he attacked the hypocrisy of the wealthy, and he devoted the proceeds of his novel *Resurrection* (1899) to help the sect of Dukhoors. His aesthetic writing reflected the importance of **morality**, but his radical Christianity resulted in his excommunication from the Russian Orthodox Church in 1901.

In *What is to be Done?* published in 1902 he urged

non-compliance with the authorities, arguing that the **power** of God transcends that of human laws.

See also: **state, equality, force**

Further reading: Gifford 1982

totalitarianism A twentieth-century concept that denotes total **power** by a **state** or group. Originally used to describe fascist regimes, it has been applied after the Second World War to regimes of the left.

The term is in essence a critique of anti-liberal regimes in which a single party rules; the gulf between state and society is erased; the individual is subject to continuous police and legal regulation; and the economy is largely controlled by the state.

A distinction is sometimes made between an authoritarian and a totalitarian regime but the difference, it could be argued, is one of degree rather than kind. Totalitarianism is simply an extreme form of authoritarianism, and the utility of the term is therefore somewhat doubtful.

It is particularly contentious to suggest that right-wing regimes are authoritarian whereas left-wing regimes are totalitarian. It is perfectly true that left-wing regimes may be autocratic in character, but to argue that an authoritarian state is totalitarian because its objectives are (however distorted) egalitarian and **emancipatory** is tendentious. Right-wing regimes may be extremely authoritarian or totalitarian, depending upon circumstances.

Moreover, while it is important not to understate the importance of liberal institutions, it is also important not to take these institutions at face value. The concentration of wealth in liberal capitalist societies means that the media, education and health care, for example, reflect vested interests and are differentially provided, so that there are greater practical limits to **freedom** in these societies than may appear at first sight.

The **state** itself, while not a totalitarian institution, does claim a monopoly of legitimate **force**. The distinction between state and society is fluid and interpenetrating, and the argument that **democracy** can be totalitarian is really an argument against an authoritarian state, rather than a serious critique of self-government.

See also: **state, emancipation, freedom**
Further reading: Arendt 1958

Trotsky, Leon (1879–1940) Born in the Ukraine and educated in Odessa. Involved in underground **politics**, he escaped from Siberia and went to London.

Here he joined the Russian Social Democratic Party but when the party split in 1903, he sided with the Mensheviks. He was leader of the St Petersburg Soviet during the abortive 1905 **revolution**, and a year later he developed his famous theory of permanent revolution, that a socialist revolution is possible in a backward country provided revolution occurs simultaneously in the advanced capitalist world. He was exiled to Siberia but escaped after two years. In 1917 he moved to the USA, but with the overthrow of the Tsar in February 1917, he returned to Russia.

Angered by Menshevik support for the Provisional Government, he joined the Bolsheviks. Trotsky became a member of the Petrograd Revolutionary Committee and played a key role in the October revolution.

He was made Peoples' Commissar for Foreign Affairs, and led the Russian delegation to negotiate with the Germans and Austrians at Brest-Litovsk. The German army resumed its advance and in March 1918, Trotsky reluctantly accepted the surrender of large swathes of Russian territory. As Commissar of War he created and led the Red Army to victory in the civil war, but his argument that the **state** should control the trade unions lost him support.

When **Stalin** became general secretary, he moved against Trotsky and his supporters. In 1927 Trotsky was expelled from the Communist Party, and two years later forced into exile. He moved to France and then Norway, publishing *My Life* in 1930, and a *History of the Russian Revolution* in 1932.

In 1937 he wrote a searing indictment of the Stalinist regime in his *Revolution Betrayed*. In 1937 he travelled to Mexico where he was assassinated on Stalin's orders in 1940.

See also: **state, Stalin**

Further reading: Thatcher 2003

Tutu, Desmond (1931–) Born in Klerksdorp, South Africa. Tutu trained first as a teacher at Pretoria Bantu Normal College and in 1954 he graduated from the University of South Africa.

In 1960 he was ordained as a priest and from 1967 to 1972, he taught theology in South Africa before returning to England as the assistant director of a theological institute in London. He published an African Prayer Book and between 1978 and 1980 he published sermons, press statements, speeches and articles in a volume entitled *Crying in the Wilderness: The Struggle for Justice in South Africa*.

He was elected a Fellow of Kings' College in 1978, and in the same year received an honorary doctorate from the General Theological Seminary in the USA. He was involved with the World Council of Churches, attending the Fifth Assembly in Nairobi in 1975 and the Sixth Assembly in Vancouver in 1983.

From 1976 to 1978 he was Bishop of Lesotho. In 1978

he became the first black General Secretary of the South African Council of Churches. In 1985–86 he was Bishop of Johannesburg, becoming Archbishop of Cape Town a year later.

In 1985 he was awarded the Nobel Peace prize in Oslo. He contributed to a volume entitled *God at 2000,* and in 1994 he published *The Rainbow People of God: The Making of a Peaceful Revolution.* He co-authored *Reconciliation: The Ubuntu Theology of Desmond Tutu* with Michael Jesse Battle, and wrote *Some Evidence of Things Seen: Children of South Africa* with Alberts and Sachs.

He chaired the investigation of the Truth and Reconciliation Commission into the crimes of apartheid. Tutu is an honorary doctor of a number of leading universities in the USA, Britain and Germany.

Further reading: Winner 1989

U

utopianism A search for an ideal society that offers a radical alternative to the current order.

Theorists divide as to whether utopias are a good or bad idea. Supporters of utopianism take the view that it is healthy to pose radical alternatives to the *status quo,* so that utopianism is a form of critique.

Critics of this view argue that utopianism can easily lead to intolerant and illiberal societies. The 'perfect' order refuses to accept imperfections and therefore inevitably creates tyrannical methods of dealing with them. Although utopias can't be realised, the attempt to bring them about can wreak havoc with our liberties. Thus, the attempt to build communism in Russia is seen as a utopian venture, creating a nightmare of bureaucracy and repression.

Some have constructed anti-utopias or dystopias. These are imaginary worlds that represent warnings either about trends in current society (carried to their logical conclusion) or statements about what could happen if a radical alternative is attempted.

Utopias can be right wing or left wing. Socialist utopias present alternatives to **capitalism** in which people work pleasurably, and joyfully accept the discipline of the collective. Right-wing utopias invariably idealise the **state**, presenting the perfect society as one run by an elite whose rule is acceptable to those upon whom it is imposed.

Marxism claims that the socialism that it advocates is 'scientific' and not 'utopian' on the grounds that it requires the maturation of capitalist contradictions to bring it about. Moreover, the communist society itself is subject to change and development. Nevertheless, **Marxism** is vulnerable to the charge of utopianism because little emphasis seems to be placed on the continuing need for **politics** even when the state itself has 'withered away'.

Utopianism is a valuable dimension to political thought, but utopians need to give thought as to how a more agreeable future can arise from a painful present.

See also: **Marxism, politics, state**
Further reading: Goodwin and Taylor 1982

utilitarianism This refers to a tradition in ethical theory that links rightness to happiness.

The theory was classically formulated by **Bentham** who argued that acts are right if they promote happiness or pleasure and wrong if they lead to misery and pain.

John Stuart **Mill** sought to modify Bentham's theory by making a distinction between different kinds of pleasure, and arguing that individuals who had experienced both higher as well as lower pleasures would always choose the former over the latter. Mill sought to link utilitarianism to development, so that individuals could change their preferences as they changed their experiences.

Critics worry that without a conception of natural **rights** the greatest happiness of the greatest number would lead to the oppression of the minority by the majority. The answer to this problem requires, it could be argued, not the notion of god-given rights, but a view of the individual that stresses the pursuit of pleasures through **relationships** with others. This would enable rightness to be judged by the happiness of individuals as they relate to one another, so that an action can only be deemed to contribute to happiness if the act of one person increases the happiness of another.

Happiness varies according to time and place. Individuals have a right to whatever can be provided to alleviate pain. Is happiness purely subjective? It appears that happiness is both subjective and objective. If it were simply subjective, then happiness could be an activity that is harmful, either to others, or to individuals themselves. If it were purely objective, then the happiness of individuals could arise from the paternalistic insistence that insists that an individual is 'really' experiencing pleasure when in fact they are in pain.

See also: **Bentham, Mill**
Further reading: Lyons 1985

V

victimhood A recent concept that suggests passivity, escapism and an unhealthy reliance on the **state** on the part of victims.

Victims are created either through acts of violence or

unforeseen mishaps like illness. Victimhood (as opposed to simply being a victim) is pathological because it involves attitudes and activities that make a bad situation even worse.

Victimhood manifests itself through a distorted analysis of the harm inflicted upon a person. For example, a victim of sexual or ethnic violence becomes prone to victimhood where they 'blame' the entire group – men or whites, for example – for the activities of a particular individual.

Moreover, victimhood is linked to passivity so that the victim does not seek practical and effective redress of the harm caused. There is an underlying pessimism to victimhood. The victim does not believe that a practical solution is possible, and hence resorts to an embittered despair. The victim of a serious illness, for example, does not seek medical help, but believes that they are simply the victim of 'fate' or have brought the misfortune upon themselves and nothing can be done about it.

Where violence is used against people, victimhood becomes a tempting albeit futile response. The state, in acting on behalf of people to either protect them or persecute them, can easily aggravate problems, and deflect victims away from an active and practical response to their difficulties.

Further reading: Lamb 1999

W

Winstanley, Gerrard (1609–76) Born in Wigan. He was a clothing apprentice when he moved to London in 1630 and became a freeman at the Merchant Taylors' Company in 1637.

The civil war broke out in 1640 and Winstanley was increasingly influenced by Lilburne and the Levellers, rejecting 'Presbyterians' and 'Independents' along with royalists.

In 1648 he published four pamphlets, arguing the case for the communal ownership of land. 'God' appears in his work as a synonym for 'Reason' and 'Babylon' represents the old order to be overthrown. His *Truth Lifting its Head above Scandals* is a fierce attack on the established clergy.

In January 1649 he published *The New Law of Righteousness* at a time when the Army had seized power. Parliament was purged, negotiations with the Levellers continued and the King had been brought to trial.

Land was taken over in Kent, Surrey, Buckinghamshire and Northamptonshire by groups calling themselves the 'Diggers', with Winstanley estimating that between a half and two thirds of the land in England was not properly cultivated, and a third of the country mere waste. Winstanley was summoned to appear before General Fairfax. Local property owners destroyed crops, huts and horses, and an action for trespass was brought against the Diggers. In July 1649 Winstanley was arrested and within a year all the Diggers' settlements had been wiped out.

In 1652 he published *The Law of Freedom* where he called upon Cromwell to redistribute land. He argued for annual elections, and for a society without money or wages.

With the restoration of the monarchy, discussion about the shape of a future England ceased. Winstanley became a Quaker and returned to London to work as a merchant.

Further reading: Hill 1976

Wollstonecraft, Mary (1759–97) Born in Spitalfields, London. In 1784 she became friends with Richard Price, a minister at the local Dissenting Chapel. At Price's home she met the publisher, Joseph Johnson, who commissioned her to write *Thoughts on the*

Education of Girls. In 1788 she helped Johnson found the *Analytical Review*.

Burke's *Reflections on the Revolution in France* was written in response to a radical sermon by Richard Price. Wollstonecraft's *A Vindication of the Rights of Man* not only supported Price but also criticised the slave trade, the game laws and the way that the poor were treated.

In 1790 she published *Vindication of the Rights of Women*. This was her classic text and makes the case for the education of women and their treatment as rational beings. As a result of this work, she was described as a 'hyena in petticoats'. In 1793 Burke led the attack on The London Corresponding Society and the Unitarian Society (both of which Wollstonecraft supported), describing them as 'loathsome insects that might, if they were allowed, grow into giant spiders as large as oxen', while King George III issued a proclamation against seditious writings and meetings.

In June 1793 Wollstonecraft decided to move to France with the American writer Gilbert Imlay. After her relationship with Imlay came to an end she returned to London. She married William **Godwin** in 1797 and soon afterwards, Mary (the author of *Frankenstein)* was born. The baby was healthy but as a result of blood poisoning, Wollstonecraft died in the same year.

See also: **Burke**

Further reading: Falco 1996

Y

Young Hegelians They were disciples of **Hegel** and sought to develop what they saw as the radical implications of his thought for **politics** and theology. This brought them into conflict with the Old or right-wing Hegelians who championed the monarchy, a bureaucratic civil service and Christianity.

The Young Hegelians emphasised Hegel's method of **dialectics**, a method, they argued, that led to **democracy**, **radicalism** and a break with religion. Both **Marx** and **Engels** were associated with the group in the early 1840s but became sharply critical of its idealist view of theory and consciousness.

Moses Hess, a communist, was also linked to the group, while *August Cieszkowski* argued that philosophy must be transcended by free, spontaneous and willed practice. **Feuerbach**'s attack on the doctrine of immortality created scandal, and *David Strauss's The Life of Jesus* argued that Jesus was an earthly being mythologised by the Church. *Bruno Bauer* further developed this case by contending that the Gospels reflected the conditions of the Roman Empire at that time, and that religion was the **alienation** of the universal self.

This theme was expanded by Feuerbach in his *Essence of Christianity*. The Young Hegelians sought to implement in Germany the French Enlightenment. They were either dismissed from university posts (like Bruno Bauer) or they failed to obtain them (like the young Marx). *Ruge* edited a Hegelian review that was targeted by the censors. Reaction was to be toppled, humanity deified, the masses spiritualised and Jews emancipated. **Stirner** identified egoism as the agent for **freedom** and **sovereignty**.

The Young Hegelians did not survive the failure of the **1848 revolutions** in Europe. Some become radical democrats; others communists; others moved to the right.

See also: **Hegel, dialectics, democracy, radicalism, Marx, Engels, Feuerbach, Stirner**
Further reading: Stepelvich 1983

Bibliography

Adair, J. (1973), *Action-centred Leadership*, Aldershot: Gower Press.

Adamson, W. (1980), *Hegemony and revolution: a Study of Antonio Gramsci's Political and Cultural Theory*, Berkeley and London: University of California Press.

Albertoni, E. (1987), *Mosca and the Theory of Elitism*, Oxford: Blackwell.

Ansell-Pearson, K. (1994), *An Introduction to Nietzsche as Political Thinker*, Cambridge: Cambridge University Press.

Arendt, H. (1958), *The Origins of Totalitarianism*, 2nd edn, New York: Meridian.

Aronson, B. (1980), *Jean-Paul Sartre: Philosophy in the World*, London: New Left Books.

Arrighi, G. et al. (1989), *Antisystemic Movements*, London and New York: Verso.

Avineri, S. (1972), *Hegel's Theory of the Modern State*, Cambridge: Cambridge University Press.

Ball, T. (1978), 'Two Concepts of Coercion', *Theory and Society*, January 1978, 97–112.

Barker, E. (1946), *The Social Contract*, London: Oxford University Press.

Baron, S. (1963), *Plekhanov, the Father of Russian Marxism*, London: Routledge and Kegan Paul.

Beechey, V. (1979), 'On Patriarchy', *Feminist Review*, 3, 66–82.

Beetham, D. (1977), 'From Socialism to Fascism: the Relation between Theory and Practice in the Work of Robert Michels', *Political Studies*, 25, 3–24, 161–81.

Beetham, D. (1991), *The Legitimation of Power*, Basingstoke: Macmillan.

Bendersky, J. (1983), *Carl Schmitt*, Princeton: Princeton University Press.

Berki, R. (1981), *On Political Realism*, London: Dent.

Bhaskar, R. (1979), *The Possibility of Naturalism: a Philosophical Critique of the Natural Sciences*, Hassocks: Harvester Press.

Biehl, J. (1997), *The Murray Bookchin Reader*, London: Cassell.

Birch, A. (1971), *Representation*, London: Pall Mall.

Bobbio, N. (1972), *On Mosca and Pareto*, Geneva: Droz.

Bouchier, D. (ed.) (1994), *Collingwood, Studies*, vol. 1, Collingwood Society: University of Wales.

Brace, L. (2004), *The Politics of Property*, Edinburgh: Edinburgh University Press.

Browning, G. (2000), *Lyotard and the End of Grand Narratives*, Cardiff: University of Wales.

Bruce, A. (1970), *Rationalism, Empiricism and Pragmatism*, New York: Random House.

Bryson, V. (1999), *Feminist Debates*, Basingstoke: Macmillan.

Bull, H. (1977), *The Anarchical Order*, Basingstoke: Macmillan.

Bulmer, M. and Rees, A. (eds) (1996), *Citizenship Today: the Contemporary Relevance of T. H. Marshall*, London: UCL Press.

Callinicos, A. (1976), *Althusser's Marxism*, London: Pluto Press.

Campbell, T. (1988), *Justice*, Basingstoke: Macmillan.

Canovan, M. (1981), *Populism*, London: Junction.

Carter, A. (1976), *Authority and Democracy*, London: Routledge and Kegan Paul.

Cassirer, E. (1982), *Kant's Life and Thought*, New Haven: Yale University Press.

Caute, D. (1970), *Fanon*, London: Fontana.

Cawson, A. (1986), *Corporatism and Political Theory*, Oxford: Blackwell.

Claudin, F. (1978), *Eurocommunism and Eurosocialism*, London: New Left Books.

Cohen, G. (1978), *Karl Marx's Theory of History: a Defence*, New Jersey: Princeton University Press.

Cole, G. D. H. (1973), *The World of Labour*, 4th edn, Brighton: Harvester.

Cole, M. (1961), *The Story of Fabian Socialism*, London: Heinemann.

Collingwood, R. (1949), *The Idea of Nature*, Oxford: Clarendon Press.

Corlett, J. A. (1991), *Equality and Liberty: analyzing Rawls and Nozick*, Basingstoke: Macmillan.

Crick, B. (1980), *George Orwell: a Life*, London: Secker and Warburg.

Croce, B. (1946), *Politics and Morals*, London: Allen and Unwin.

Crosland, S. (1982), *Tony Crosland*, London: Cape.

Cunningham, N. (1987), *In Pursuit of Reason: the Life of Thomas Jefferson*, London: Louisiana State University Press.

Dahl, R. (1961), *Who Governs?*, New Haven: Yale University Press.

Davies, T. (1997), *Humanism*, London: Routledge.

Deutscher, I. (1966), *Stalin: a Political Biography*, Harmondsworth: Penguin.

Drinnon, R. (1970), *Rebel in Paradise: a Biography of Emma Goldman*, Boston, MA: Beacon Press.

Duchêne, F. (1994), *Jean Monnet: the First Statesman of Independence*, New York and London: Norton.

Dunant, S. (ed.) (1994), *The War of the Words: the Political Correctness Debate*, London: Virago.

Dunleavy, P. and O'Leary, B. (1987), *Theories of the State*, Basingstoke: Macmillan.

Dworkin, A. and MacKinnon, C. (1988), *Pornography and Civil Rights: a New Day for Women's Equality*, Minneapolis: Organizing Against Pornography.

Easton, D. (1953/1971), *The Political System: An Inquiry into the State of Political Science*, 2nd edn, New York: Alfred Knopf.

Easton, D. (1965), *A Framework for Political Analysis*, New Jersey: Prentice Hall.

Engels, F. (1964), *The Dialectics of Nature*, Moscow: Progress Publishers.

Engels, F. (1968), 'Ludwig Feuerbach and the End of German Classical Philosophy', in Marx Engels, *Selected Works*, London: Lawrence and Wishart.

Epstein, D. (1984), *The Political Theory of 'The Federalist'*, Chicago: University of Chicago Press.

Etzioni, A. (1996), *The New Golden Rule*, London: Profile Books.

Evans, D. and Jenkins, J. (1999), *Years of Weimar and the Third Reich*, London: Hodder and Stoughton.

Falco, M. (1996), *Feminist Interpretations of Mary Wollstonecraft*, Pennsylvania: Pennsylvania State University Press.

Faulks, K. (2000), *Citizenship*, New York and London: Routledge.

Femia, J. (1981), *Gramsci's Political Thought*, Oxford: Clarendon Press.

Fenn, R. (1987), *James Mill's Political Thought*, New York and London: Garland.

Finley, M. (1980), *Ancient Slavery and Modern Ideology*, London: Chatto and Windus.

Flathman, R. (1966), *The Public Interest*, New York: Wiley.

Foley, M. (2000), *The British Presidency: Tony Blair and the Politics of Public Leadership*, Manchester: Manchester University Press.

Fromm, E. (1956), *The Sane Society*, London: Routledge and Kegan Paul.

Gay, P. (1962), *The Dilemma of Democratic Socialism*, New York: Collier.

Geary, D. (1987), *Karl Kautsky*, Manchester: Manchester University Press.

Geohegan, V. (1981), *Reason and Eros: the Social Theory of Herbert Marcuse*, London: Pluto.

Geras, N. (1976), *The Legacy of Rosa Luxemburg*, London: Verso.

Giddens, A. (1998), *The Third Way*, Cambridge: Polity Press.

Gifford, H. (1982), *Tolstoy*, Oxford: Oxford University Press.

Goodwin, B. and Taylor, K. (1982), *The Politics of Utopia*, London: Hutchinson.

Gough, J. (1973), *John Locke's Political Philosophy*, Oxford: Clarendon Press.

Gray, J. (1984), *Hayek on Liberty*, Oxford: Robertson.

Gray, J. (1996), *Isaiah Berlin*, New Jersey: Princeton University Press.

Gray, T. (1990), *Freedom*, London: Macmillan.

Greenleaf, W. (1965), *Oakeshott's Philosophical Politics*, London: Longman.

Greer, G. (1999), *The Whole Woman*, London: Transworld Publishers.

Guest, S. (ed.) (1996), *Positivism Today*, Aldershot: Dartmouth.

Harding, N. (1981), *Lenin's Political Thought*, vol. 1; *Theory and Practice in the Socialist Revolution*, vol. 2, Basingstoke: Macmillan.

Harding, N. (1996), *Leninism*, Basingstoke: Macmillan.

Haugaard, M. (ed.) (2002), *Power: A Reader*, Manchester and New York: Manchester University Press.

Held, D. (1987), *Models of Democracy*, 2nd edn, Cambridge: Polity Press.

Hill, C. (ed.) (1976), *Winstanley: the Law of Freedom and Other Essays*, Harmondsworth: Penguin.

Hoffman, J. (1975), *Marxism and the Theory of Praxis*, London: Lawrence and Wishart.

Hoffman, J. (1995), *Beyond the State*, Cambridge: Polity Press.

Hoffman, J. (1998), *Sovereignty*, Buckingham: Open University Press.

Hoffman, J. (2001), *Gender and Sovereignty*, Basingstoke: Palgrave.

Hoffman, J. (2004), *Citizenship Beyond the State*, London: Sage.

Horton, J. and Mendus, S. (eds) (1999), *Toleration, Identity and Difference*, Basingstoke: Macmillan.

Hughes, C. (2002), *Feminist Theory and Research*, London: Sage.

Hutchinson, J. and Smith, A. D. (eds) (1994), *Nationalism*, Oxford: Oxford University Press.

Ignatieff, M. (1985), *The Needs of Strangers*, New York: Viking.

Ionescu, G. (ed.) (1976), *The Political Thought of Saint-Simon*, London: Oxford University Press.

Iyer, R. (1973), *The Moral and Political Thought of Mahatma Gandhi*, New York: Oxford University Press.

Jordan, B. (1989), *The Common Good: Citizenship, Morality and Self-Interest*, Oxford: Blackwell.

Kellner, D. (1989), *Jean Baudrillard: From Marxism to Postmodernism and Beyond*, Cambridge: Polity Press.

Laclau, E. (1966), *Emancipation(s)*, London: Verso.

Lamb, S. (ed.) (1999), *New Versions of Victims*, New York and London: New York University Press.

Laqueur, W. (2003), *No End to War*, New, York and London: Continuum.

Leftwich, A. (ed.) (1994), *What is Politics?*, Oxford: Blackwell.

Levitas, R. (1986), *The Ideology of the New Right*, Cambridge: Polity Press.

Lindley, R. (1986), *Autonomy*, Basingstoke: Macmillan.

Lively, J. (1962), *The Social and Political Thought of Alexis de Tocqueville*, Oxford: Clarendon Press.

Long, P. (1969), *The New Left*, Boston, MA: Porter Sergeant.

Löwy, M. (1979), *Georg Lukács: from Romanticism to Bolshevism*, London: New Left Books.

Lukes, S. (1973), *Individualism*, Oxford: Blackwell.

Lyons, D. (1985), *Forms and Limits of Utilitarianism*, Oxford: Oxford University Press.

Lyons, J. (1970), *Chomsky*, London: Fontana.

MacIntyre, A. (1981), *After Virtue*, Notre Dame, Indiana: University of Notre Dame Press.

MacKinnon, C. (1989), *Toward a Feminist Theory of the State*, Cambridge, MA: Harvard University Press.

McLellan, D. (1969), *The Young Hegelians and Karl Marx*, New York: Praeger.

McLellan, D. (1977), *Engels*, Glasgow: Fontana.

McLellan, D. (1979), *Marxism After Marx*, Basingstoke: Macmillan.

McLellan, D. (1995), *Ideology*, 2nd edn, Buckingham: Open University Press.

McLellan, D. (2000), *Karl Marx: Selected Writings*, Oxford: Oxford University Press.

McLennan, G. (1995), *Pluralism*, Buckingham: Open University Press.

Macpherson, C. B. (1982), *Burke*, Oxford: Oxford University Press.

Maehl, W. (1980), *August Bebel, Shadow Emperor of the German Workers*, Philadelphia: American Philosophical Society.

Magee, B. (1973), *Popper*, London: Fontana.

Maheu, A.(ed.) (1995), *Social Movements and Social Classes*, London: Sage.

Marshall, P. (1984), *William Godwin*, New Haven: Yale University Press.

Marshall, P. (1993), *Demanding the Impossible*, London: HarperCollins.

Mieksins Wood, E. and Wood, N. (1978), *Class Ideology and Political Theory: Socrates, Plato and Aristotle*, Oxford: Blackwell.

Miller, D. (1981), *Philosophy and Ideology in Hume's Political Thought*, Oxford: Clarendon Press.

Miller, J. and Vincent, R. (eds) (1990), *Order and Violence: Hedley Bull and International Relations*, Oxford: Clarendon.

Miller, M. (1976), *Kropotkin*, Chicago: University of Chicago Press.

Millett, K. (1977), *Sexual Politics*, London: Virago.

Mulgan, R. (1977), *Aristotle's Political Theory*, Oxford: Oxford University Press.

Murray, M. (1978), *Heidegger and Modern Philosophy*, New Haven: Yale University Press.

Morton, A. L. (1969), *The Life and Ideas of Robert Owen*, London: Lawrence and Wishart.

Newman, M. (2004), *Ralph Miliband and the Politics of the New Left*, London: Verso. P. Nicholson (1984), 'Politics and Force', in A. Leftwich (ed.), *What is Politics?*, Oxford: Blackwell.

Nolte, E. (1969), *Three Faces of Fascism*, New York: New American Library.

Norman, R. and Sayers, S. (1980), *Hegel, Marx and Dialectic*, Brighton: Harvester.

Oliver, D. (1999), *Common Values and the Public-Private Divide*, London: Butterworths.

O'Neill, J. (1998), *The Market: Ethics, Knowledge and Politics*, New York, Routledge.

Outhwaite, W. (1994), *Habermas: a Critical Introduction*, Cambridge: Polity Press.

Parekh, B. (ed.) (1974), *Jeremy Bentham: Ten Critical Essays*, London: Cass.

Parekh, B. (1981), *Hannah Arendt and the Search for a New Political Philosophy*, Basingstoke: Macmillan.

Parekh, B. (2000), *Rethinking Multiculturalism*, Basingstoke: Macmillan.

Parry, G. (1969), *Political Elites*, London: Allen and Unwin.

Pateman, C. (1981), *The Sexual Contract*, Cambridge: Polity Press.

Pateman, C. (1985), *The Problem of Political Obligation*, Cambridge: Polity Press.

Pennock, J. and Chapman, J. (eds) (1976), *Nomos IX: Equality*, New York: Atherton.

Peterson, S. (ed.) (1992), *Gendered States*, Boulder, Co: Lynne Reiner.

Pettit, P. (1975), *The Concept of Structuralism: a Critical Analysis*, Berkeley: University of California Press.

Pettit, P. (1997), *Republicanism*, Oxford: Oxford University Press.

Porritt, J. (1984), *Seeing Green: the Politics of Ecology Explained*, Oxford: Blackwell.

Porter, C. (1980), *Alexandra Kollontai: a Biography*, London: Virago.

Raimondo, J. (2000), *An Enemy of the State: The Life of Murray N. Rothbard*, New York: Prometheus Books.

Ramsey, M. (1997), *What's Wrong with Liberalism?*, London and Washington: Leicester University Press.

Raphael, D. (1977), *Hobbes*, London: Allen and Unwin.

Raphael, D. (1985), *Adam Smith*, Oxford: Oxford University Press.

Richter, M. (1964), *The Politics of Conscience: T. H. Green and his Age*, London and Cambridge: Weidenfeld and Nicolson.

Richter, M. (ed.) (1977), *The Political Theory of Montesquieu*, Cambridge: Cambridge University Press.

Roazen, P. (1968), *Freud: Political and Social Thought*, New York: Vintage.

Ryan, A. (1974), *J. S. Mill*, London and Boston, MA: Routledge and Kegan Paul.

Sanders, P. (1995), *Capitalism*, Buckingham: Open University Press.

Sayer, D. (1987), *The Violence of Abstraction*, Oxford: Blackwell.

Schram, S. (1983), *Mao Zedong: A Preliminary Assessment*, Hong Kong: Chinese University Press.

Sheridan, A. (1980), *Michel Foucault: the Will to Truth*, London: Tavistock.

Shklar, J. (1969), *Men and Citizens: a Study of Rousseau's Social Theory*, London: Cambridge University Press.

Singer, P. (1977), *Animal Liberation*, New York: Avon.

Skinner, Q. (1981), *Machiavelli*, Oxford: Oxford University Press.

Skocpol, T. (1979), *States and Social Revolutions*, Cambridge: Cambridge University Press.

Stanley, J. (1981), *The Sociology of Virtue: the Political and Social Theories of Georges Sorel*, Berkeley: University of California Press.

Stepelvich, L. (ed.) (1983), *The Young Hegelians: an Anthology*, Cambridge: Cambridge University Press.

Stiglitz, J. (2002), *Globalization and its Discontents*, London: Allen Lane Penguin.

Tawney, R. (1969), *Religion and the Rise of Capitalism*, Harmondsworth: Penguin.

Taylor, M. (1982), *Community, Anarchy and Liberty*, Cambridge: Cambridge University Press.

Thatcher, I. (2003), *Trotsky*, London and New York: Routledge.

Tilman, R. (1984), *C. Wright Mills: a Native Radical and his American Intellectual Roots*, Philadelphia: Pennsylvania State University Press.

Townshend, J. (2000), *C. B. Macpherson and the Problem of Liberal Democracy*, Edinburgh: Edinburgh University Press.

Tucker, K. (1998), *Anthony Giddens and Modern Social Theory*, London: Sage.

Tucker, R. (ed.) (1978), *The Marx–Engels Reader*, 2nd edn, New York and London: Norton.

Waldron, J. (1984), *Theories of Rights*, Oxford: Oxford University Press.

Warren, B. (1980), *Imperialism: Pioneer of Capitalism*, London: New Left.

Wartofsky, M. (1977), *Feuerbach*, Cambridge: Cambridge University Press.

Willets, D. (1992), *Modern Conservatism*, Harmondsworth: Penguin.

Williamson, A. (1973), *Thomas Paine: His Life, Work and Time*, London: Allen and Unwin.

Winner, D. (1989), *Desmond Tutu*, Watford: Exley.

Wolfreys, J. (1998), *Deconstruction: Derrida*, Basingstoke: Macmillan.

Woodcock, G. (1956), *Pierre-Joseph Proudhon: a Biography*, New York: Macmillan.

Woods, T. (1999), *Beginning Postmodernism*, Manchester: Manchester University Press.

Woolf, R. (1977), *Understanding Rawls*, New Jersey: Princeton University Press.

Wright, E. (1985), *Classes*, London: Verso.

Yolton, J. (2000), *Realism and Appearances*, Cambridge: Cambridge University Press.

Young, H. (1991), *One of Us: a Biography of Margaret Thatcher*, Basingstoke: Macmillan.